Map from Classroom Atlas, 1994 Edition,
© 1995 by Rand McNally, 94-S-268

Longitude West of Greenwich Longitude East of Greenwich

20° 4 10° 5 0° 6 10° 7 20° 8 30° 9 40° 10 50° 11 60°

A-580000-21 -15·23·55
COSMO SERIES AFRICA
Copyright by
RAND McNALLY & COMPANY
Made in U.S.A.

0 200 400 600 800 1000 Miles

Sinusoidal Projection
SCALE 1:36,313,000 1 Inch = 565 Statute Miles

Enchantment of the World

MOZAMBIQUE

By Jason Lauré and Ettagale Blauer

Consultant for Mozambique: Nelson Francisco de Carvalho, M.A., Instructor of African Literature and Culture, Stanford University, Stanford, California

Consultant for Reading: Robert L. Hillerich, Ph.D., Professor Emeritus, Bowling Green State University; Consultant, Pinellas County Schools, Florida

CHILDRENS PRESS ®

CHICAGO

A village in Maputo Province

Project Editor: Mary Reidy
Design: Margrit Fiddle
Photo Research: Feldman & Associates, Inc.

Library of Congress Cataloging-in-Publication Data

Lauré, Jason.
   Mozambique / by Jason Lauré and Ettagale Blauer..
      p.   cm.—(Enchantment of the world)
   Includes index.
   Summary: Discusses the history, geography, people,
and culture of the southeast African nation that is just
recovering from a civil war and a severe drought.
   ISBN 0-516-02636-4
   1. Mozambique—Juvenile literature. I. Blauer,
Ettagale. II. Title. III. Series.
DT3299.L38   1995   95-2690
967.9—dc20   CIP
                                                AC

Picture Acknowledgments
AP/Wide World Photos: 35 (right), 39 (3 photos), 53 (left)
The Bettmann Archive: 17 (right), 19, 34
Lauré Communications: © **Jason Lauré,** 4, 5, 8, 9, 11, 12, 15,
24, 27, 35 (left), 44, 45, 56 (3 photos), 58 (4 photos), 60 (2
photos), 62, 65, 67, 70, 71 (2 photos), 72 (2 photos), 73, 82
(left), 84 (2 photos), 85, 88, 90, 91 (3 photos), 92 (2 photos),
93, 99, 100 (2 photos), 103 (left inset), 104, 106 (top, bottom
right), 108; © **Michael Teague,** 33; © **Alfredo Mueche,** 49,
106 (bottom left); © **Joel Chiziane,** 50, 69, 82 (right), 87;
© **Antonio Muchave,** 68 (left), 79, 86, 95; © **Anders Nilsson,**
68 (right), 83 (left), 97
North Wind Picture Archives: 14, 17 (left), 22, 23
Photri: 103
Reuters/Bettmann: 47, 51, 53 (right), 76
Stock Montage: 26
Tony Stone Images: © **Brian Seed,** Cover, 6, 78 (2 photos),
109; © **Penny Tweedie,** 61
UPI/Bettmann Newsphotos: 31, 41 (2 photos), 94
Valan: © **Jean-Marie Jro,** 103 (right inset)
Len W. Meents: Maps on 89, 94
Courtesy Flag Research Center, Winchester,
Massachusetts 01890: Flag on back cover
Cover: Women rest on the steps of Misericordia Church,
        Ihla de Moçambique

The port of Maputo with the skyline of the city in the background

TABLE OF CONTENTS

A tea plantation in the western hills

Chapter 1

NATURAL ENVIRONMENT AND PEOPLE

The Republic of Mozambique stretches for 1,556 miles (2,504 kilometers) along the southeastern coast of Africa, facing the Indian Ocean. In land area Mozambique occupies 308,642 square miles (799,384 square kilometers), and is nearly twice the size of California, with a similar, elongated shape.

The country's northern border is the Rovuma River, which separates Mozambique from Tanzania. Its western border is more complicated. Mozambique is formed in the shape of an irregular "Y," with the eastern arm of the "Y," being taller and broader than the other. In between the two arms of the "Y" lies the nation of Malawi. The other nations to the west of Mozambique are Zambia, Zimbabwe, South Africa, and Swaziland. The westernmost part of Mozambique, the other arm of the "Y," is set along both sides of the Zambezi River. The widest part of the country is in the north, the eastern arm of the "Y," where it extends from the Indian Ocean to Lake Malawi, also called Lake Nyasa. The narrowest part is the extreme southern end of the country, next to Swaziland, where it measures about fifty miles (eighty kilometers) across.

Nearly half of all the land in Mozambique is low lying, including the shores of the sixty rivers that run through it, as well

Marshy lowlands near Maputo

as the long oceanfront strip. Much of the low-lying land is marshy and not suitable for most agricultural uses. This moist region is a good breeding ground for insects, including mosquitoes and tsetse flies that carry sleeping sickness, which affects both people and livestock in much of the northern part of the country.

Parts of Mozambique are marked by sharply rising hills, steep slopes, and low plateaus. The western part of the country and the region north of the Zambezi valley are marked by a series of highlands. The highest point in the country is Mount Binga, which rises to 7,992 feet (2,436 meters) in the highlands area known as the Manica escarpment.

A view of the highlands from the Zambezi River

RIVERS

Mozambique is crossed by several major rivers and dozens of smaller ones, and these have played an important role in the country's development. The Zambezi River, which runs across much of the continent of Africa, enters the country from the west and flows to the east, eventually entering the Indian Ocean, as do all of Mozambique's rivers. The Zambezi effectively separates the nation into halves, forming a natural barrier to travel from southern to northern Mozambique.

The other major rivers running across Mozambique from west to east include the Lurio, the Save, and the Limpopo. Although the Limpopo is the largest of these rivers, it is a slow-moving stream except during flood tide, a time when it catches the runoff from the region's seasonal rains. Because of the extensive wetlands, it is difficult for people to move across the country.

As is true in much of Africa, the flow of water in the rivers varies greatly, depending on whether it is the dry or the rainy season. The runoff from seasonal rains reaches its high point between January and March and its low point between June and August. As the dry season progresses, some rivers disappear completely, leaving only the riverbed as an indication that there was ever any water there. When the rains begin, the riverbed can fill up in a matter of hours.

Until the construction of the Cabora Bassa Dam on the Zambezi River, which resulted in the formation of a large lake, Mozambique had no permanent body of freshwater within its boundaries. The only accessible large body of water was Lake Malawi.

CLIMATE

The weather in Mozambique is divided into dry and wet seasons, rather than warm and cool seasons. In a normal year, more than 80 percent of the entire year's rain falls during the wet season, which in most parts of the country usually starts in October and lasts through March. For the remaining six months of the year, there may be only a trace of rain. Most of the people in Mozambique are farmers, so irrigation plays an important role in seeing the people through the dry season.

Amounts of rainfall vary in different parts of the country, with most areas receiving between 47 to 79 inches (119 to 201 centimeters). Very few regions get more than 79 inches (201 centimeters). In a large portion of the southwest, between the Save and Limpopo Rivers, less than 16 inches (41 centimeters) of rain falls each year. Drought is frequent, especially in the south,

Ancient San rock paintings

and can have a devastating effect on the crops, resulting in widespread famine. This happened in the early 1980s when there was a massive crop failure.

While the humidity and temperature are generally higher than average during the rainy season, the climate in Mozambique is usually pleasant, with temperatures ranging from 68 to 85 degrees Fahrenheit (20 to 29.4 degrees Celsius). Along the coast, ocean breezes make the warmer months more pleasant.

THE EARLIEST PEOPLE

The first people who lived in present-day Mozambique were small bands of hunters and gatherers such as Khoi and San. Many people called them Bushmen. They hunted wild animals using

Hunters and gatherers were the first people living in present-day Mozambique.

bows and arrows tipped with poisons they made from plants. They also ate roots, berries, and other foods they found. Instead of establishing permanent settlements, they survived by living and moving around in small groups. Until about the fourth century A.D., they were the only human occupants of the land.

As people began moving into the region from the north and west of Mozambique, the Khoi and San either moved out or lost their distinctive characteristics through intermarriage with the newcomers. These black Africans, who moved in steadily over a period of several hundred years, depended on agriculture and were looking for land they could farm.

AFRICAN MIGRATIONS

By the fourteenth century the African people who migrated from central Africa into Mozambique included the *Maravi*, a strong warrior people, who settled in the area that includes the present-day country of Malawi. The Maravi were among the earliest traders in the region, dealing with the Arab merchants who came to Mozambique in sailing ships called *dhows*. The Maravi brought ivory from the interior of Africa as far as the Zambezi River. Then the Arabs, using the Zambezi as their "highway," transported the ivory by boat to the natural harbors on the Indian Ocean. The coastline of Mozambique had many of these harbors where boats could tie up and be loaded. These harbors are a natural part of Mozambique's irregularly shaped coastline and were developed into ports many years later.

The Maravi took over the land of other people who had lived in the region for about four hundred years. Among these people were the Macua-Lomue, a name that includes a number of different ethnic groups. The Macua-Lomue lived in village groups north of the Zambezi River under the guidance of a chief and a council of elders.

Much farther north, close to the border of present-day Tanzania, lived the Makonde and the Yao. Because they occupied such a remote region, the Makonde remained out of reach of most other people, including the Arabs and the Portuguese. The Yao began moving to the south to facilitate trade with the Arabs.

SHONA-SPEAKING PEOPLE

South of the Zambezi River, the major language group was the Shona-speaking people, who had settled vast areas of the region by the tenth and eleventh centuries. They would become one of the largest groups in the territory, which included present-day Zimbabwe.

Arab traders sailed in ships called dhows.

The people known as the Tsonga continued to expand their settlements in southern Mozambique until they came into contact with the Portuguese. The Tsonga and other dominant groups introduced their customs to the people they conquered as well as to those they lived among. In this way cultures were changed and sometimes strengthened.

ARAB TRADERS

Mozambique's long coastline and natural harbors made it both attractive and accessible to cultures that would play crucial roles in its development. The first to come were the Arab traders who had mastered the art of sailing with the shifting currents of the Indian Ocean along the African coast. In their graceful dhows, they made the long trip from the Arabian Peninsula. By the eighth century they had already established trading posts along the East African coast. Sofala, south of the Zambezi River, was a port town that was developed by the Arab traders.

A woman of mixed African and Arab ancestry

Although Mozambique's interior is hard to cross, the Arabs made their way inland. Manufactured goods—mostly ceramics, cloth, and glass—as well as salt, a precious item used to preserve food, were brought by the Arabs. They also brought guns, a new kind of weapon that was highly desired by the chiefs in their ongoing battles with other African peoples. They traded these products for the natural products of Africa—gold, palm oil, and especially, ivory.

The influence of the Arab traders extended all along the African coast, with Mozambique as the southernmost point. The Arabs were Muslims and brought their religion, Islam, with them. Arabs mixed with the African people and through intermarriage created a new culture known as *Swahili*, which means "coastal" in the Arabic language. The Swahili culture extends for hundreds of miles along the African coastline and the Swahili language is spoken by millions of people in different East African countries. The name Mozambique is thought to come from *Musa al Big*, the name of an Arab *sheikh*, "chief," who lived on Ihla de Moçambique.

Chapter 2

EXPLORATION AND
THE PORTUGUESE

AGE OF DISCOVERY

The explorers who sailed from Portugal, a country located on the southwestern edge of Europe on the Atlantic Ocean, were the most skilled navigators of their day. Their knowledge of the ocean currents and their understanding of how to make use of the winds enabled them to travel the world in their small boats, called *caravels*. They were sent out by the kings of Portugal with a mission to explore the largely unknown regions beyond their shores.

Their goals were spices and gold. Spices were known to come from the East, and the explorers were prepared to sail halfway around the world to find them. Spices were used to preserve food, especially meat and fish, in the days before the invention of refrigeration. The captains on these voyages also had another mission: to expand the influence of Christianity in the face of a growing Muslim presence in their part of the world.

In 1497 King Manuel the Fortunate of Portugal sent the explorer Vasco da Gama on a voyage to find a better route to India, the source of the spices. Vasco da Gama sailed south through the

Vasco da Gama (left) used ships with many sails (right) to catch the wind.

Atlantic Ocean, went around Africa at the Cape of Winds, which he renamed the Cape of Good Hope, and into the Indian Ocean. A year after he set sail, da Gama and his crew stopped briefly in Delagoa Bay on the southern coast of Mozambique. They reached the Muslim town of Ilha de Moçambique, a small island off the coast of Mozambique, in 1498. Vasco da Gama moved on to his ultimate destination, India, but he opened the route for others who would follow him to Mozambique.

The Portuguese saw the riches that had been developed by Arab traders. Africa offered gold and ivory; the Portuguese traded cloth, beads, and guns in exchange. With their superior guns and navigation, the Portuguese quickly overpowered the Arab boats and their crews and set about establishing military control of the coastal region of Mozambique. The Portuguese were brutal in their methods; whenever an Arab sheikh offered the slightest opposition, the Portuguese either burned the town or bombarded it from the sea. The Arabs of the coastal settlements soon learned that they must agree to the Portuguese terms and pay them for the right to continue to live and do business in the region.

CONTROL OF THE COASTAL TRADE

By 1510, just twelve years after they first touched the shore of Mozambique, the Portuguese were in control of the trade of every coastal town between Sofala in Mozambique and Mogadishu in Somalia, thousands of miles to the north. Unlike the Arab traders who traveled into the interior, they relied on people bringing the goods to them. To protect this trade they built a series of forts. It was the pattern of these sailing explorers to build forts wherever they reached a desirable point of land. The stone for the forts came with them from Portugal—used as ballast in their ships on the outward journey. They did not need the ballast on the trip back because their ships were loaded with goods.

But it soon became clear that to control the coastal trade, forts would not be enough. The Portuguese would have to control the people in the interior as well. The Portuguese would have to leave the coastal region they knew and make their way inland.

EXPLORING THE INTERIOR

Early Portuguese explorations of the interior of the land began in 1515. The desire to control trade, especially the gold from the mines at Great Zimbabwe and other sites, led to conflict. The Portuguese were able to subdue the Shona (who lived in present-day Zimbabwe) and eventually became the Shona's allies, fighting with them against other groups. Over the next century, through military action as well as by making trade deals, the Portuguese

The Portuguese built this fort around 1558.

obtained the rights to large land areas. These were turned over to Portuguese settlers who began arriving at the beginning of the seventeenth century. According to Portuguese law, the settlers won the rights to more than the land itself. They also had the rights to use the African people who lived on the land. The African people were forced to work for the Portuguese on their *fazendas*, large agricultural estates, and to mine the gold that was found in the region.

TAKING OVER THE LAND

The Portuguese established a pattern of granting control of the land to the *prazeiros*, the leaseholders or landlords, and taking the land's resources without improving it. The prazeiros created armies of slaves to protect these land and mineral holdings in the interior of Africa. The slaves traded away their freedom for the protection the Portuguese offered. They needed to be protected from other, more warlike Africans.

The Portuguese rulers expected to benefit from the work of the prazeiros without spending any of the resources of the Portuguese kingdom. However, the prazeiros were more interested in creating profits for themselves, and Portugal soon found that it had lost control of its landholdings in Mozambique.

AFRICAN OPPOSITION

Portuguese supremacy was challenged by other Africans fighting among themselves. The Portuguese tried to take advantage of this hostility by playing one side against the other. Among the strongest were the Shona, who were ruled by a *mambo*, or high chief. The mambo was believed to have special powers and his soldiers were able to defeat the *monomutapa*, the region's most important leader.

By the beginning of the eighteenth century, Portuguese influence in Mozambique had been reduced to a few small areas of control. The Portuguese now were trying to gain the benefits of trade without having to actually control the huge land areas and the people of the territory.

Although the Portuguese were being pushed out of the territory, they had created a legacy that would endure—the prazeiros had intermarried with African women and created a mixed-race society. These people, known as *mestiços*, "mixed," carried Portuguese family names but maintained their African culture. (The more commonly used word is the Spanish *mestizo*.) The mestiços ran the estates that the Portuguese had hoped would provide profits for the home country.

By the eighteenth century most of the estates had been abandoned or were no longer producing any wealth. Mozambique was a harsh place for both Europeans and Africans. Malaria and other tropical diseases claimed many lives, including some of the land-hungry settlers who traveled there from Portugal. The great hope that Mozambique could be turned into profitable farming estates remained a dream.

It was not until the late 1700s that Portugal gained control of the most important port along the Mozambique coast. First known as Delagoa Bay, it was later named Lourenço Marques in recognition of the Portuguese explorer who first noted its existence. Today it is known as Maputo, the capital city, while the bay is still called Delagoa Bay.

These early experiences in Mozambique did not deter the Portuguese from wanting to control the territory. Portugal had few financial resources to invest in its African landholdings, yet it had become dependent on the people and products it took from Africa.

The Portuguese saw themselves as equal to the other European nations that had colonial holdings in Africa. And so they held on to Mozambique and their other African holdings long after there was any chance of making a profit from them. There are five former Portuguese colonies in Africa: Mozambique, Angola, Cape Verde, São Tomé and Príncipe, and Guinea-Bissau.

THE SLAVE TRADE

The idea of one human being owning another, of taking people away from their homes and forcing them to work, is an ancient one. There was "internal" slavery in Africa long before Europeans

The slave traders selected young and healthy Africans.

arrived. These slaves frequently were captured in war and turned into workers. They often wound up living close to their original homelands because their captors were from nearby villages or territories.

Taking people totally out of their environment and shipping them thousands of miles away was a new idea. It became one of the biggest economic activities for the Portuguese in Africa. The prazeiros made the trade possible in Mozambique. They were familiar with the interior and had many people working for them who could guide the slaves to the coast where the ships were waiting. It is estimated that by 1790, about nine thousand slaves were sent out of Mozambique each year. This represented a large portion of the local population and had far-ranging effects. The most desirable slaves were those who were young and strong— the heart of the community. Those least able to take care of themselves, the children and the elderly, were left behind. Slavery severely disrupted and altered the development of African cultures.

An African chief sells his prisoners of war to a slave dealer.

Not every European nation was equally involved in the slave trade. By the early 1800s the British had enacted laws against slavery and were patrolling the seas, trying to stop the boats that were transporting slaves. Most of the British patrols were off the *west* coast of Africa, in the Atlantic Ocean, and this left the *east* coast of Africa, where Mozambique is located, unprotected. As a result, the slave trade from Mozambique actually grew during this period. Most of these slaves were transported around the southern tip of Africa, around the Cape of Good Hope, and on to plantations in Brazil, at that time a Portuguese colony in South America.

When a treaty was signed between Britain and Portugal in 1844 allowing officers from Britain's Royal Navy to inspect Portuguese ships, the slave trade dropped considerably. However, many ship captains smuggled shipments of slaves. Some trade continued for many years, even after Portugal outlawed slavery in 1878.

A reenactment of one of the major battles of the Zulu in southern Africa—the Battle of Isandhlwana

FIGHTING THE ZULU NATION

One of the greatest challenges to Portuguese control of Mozambique was presented by the Zulu people, led by the powerful warrior Shaka and his brother Dingane. Shaka's fierce attacks were responsible for reshaping the cultural map of southern Africa. The Zulu warriors, under Shaka's leadership, set out to rule or crush all the people in the region. As the Zulus approached, many people simply fled from their villages. Those who remained were attacked and then made part of the Zulu kingdom. Today many Zulu live right next to Mozambique, in the region of South Africa called Maputoland.

Even with their advanced guns and other weapons, the Portuguese were defeated by the Zulu, who captured the fort at the town of Lourenço Marques in 1833. The Zulu even caused the British to suffer their only defeat at the hands of African troops, at the Battle of Isandhlwana in 1879.

Those who escaped from Shaka's rule used many of his methods themselves. They raided villages, took the livestock, and carried off the women, who then became part of their group. One of the most successful groups who broke away was the Ngoni. They later became known as the Shangaan people. In 1895 Gungunhana, chief of the Vatuas (an ethnic group of Zulus), battled Portuguese troops. He fought fiercely and was the hero of his age. Eventually he was defeated and sent to live in exile in the distant Azores islands, another Portuguese colony.

EXPANDING COLONIAL RULE

The role of the prazeiros grew smaller, although a few families now controlled vast estates in the area around the Zambezi River. These estates were quite independent from the rest of the territory. The families, many of them mestiço, lived completely African lives in their customs and even in their language. This kind of integration into an African culture was unique among the European peoples.

As the Europeans in neighboring territories began to take greater control of their lands, no international group recognized Portuguese authority over Mozambique. The British, in particular, were claiming vast regions to the south of Mozambique and threatening Portuguese claims. Unlike the Portuguese, the British were actively ruling the areas they claimed and used this as justification for their rights to the region. In 1875 a major dispute between them was settled in favor of Portugal. Recognition was given to Portugal's "right" to the region of southern Mozambique.

A Portuguese gunboat on the Zambezi River

DIVIDING UP AFRICA

As the nineteenth century drew to a close, European claims to various territories in Africa came into conflict. In an effort to settle these claims peacefully and prevent the European powers from going to war over their African land claims, a conference was held in 1885-1886, in Berlin. One of the basic ways to establish a claim was to show that there was sufficient settlement of Europeans in the territory to claim occupation. The Portuguese didn't meet this requirement because they occupied little of Mozambique. Essentially, they had control over part of the coast, part of the Zambezi River basin, and the port of Lourenço Marques, which they only recently had taken from the Zulu. In spite of their shaky hold over the region, the Portuguese actually claimed a piece of land stretching across Africa, from the Atlantic Ocean to the Indian Ocean, connecting Mozambique in the east with Angola in the west.

By the time the conference ended, all the major European

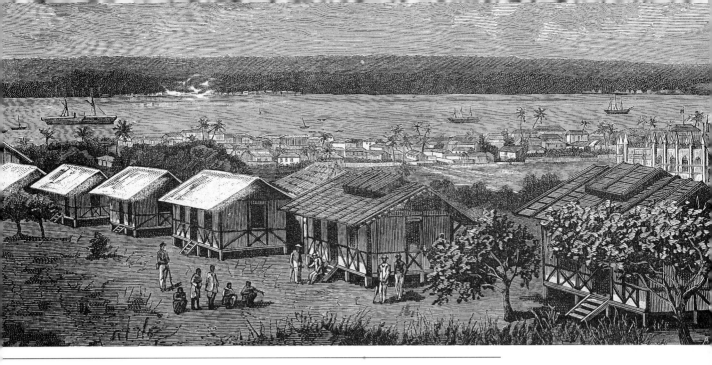

A hospital built by the Portuguese at Lourenço Marques in the 1880s

powers except Britain had agreed to recognize Portugal's claims over Mozambique. Britain especially objected to Portugal's coast-to-coast claim. Small wars were fought along the disputed boundaries until 1891, when Portugal was forced to agree to Britain's claim to the region of Mashonaland, part of present-day Zimbabwe.

Portugal's claim to the interior of Mozambique, however, required warfare against the people of the Zambezi region, which continued into the early years of the twentieth century. Little by little the Portuguese began to control the regions they claimed, but their actual administration of the territory was limited. The governor-general, who lived in Lourenço Marques, was officially in charge, but he had little real control or even knowledge of what was going on in the sprawling colony.

To establish a presence in the distant northern section of Mozambique, Portugal had to subdue the Makua and the Makonde, as well as the Yao people. Not until 1912 were the Portuguese able to set up trading posts in the northern region.

27

Chapter 3

TWENTIETH-CENTURY COLONIALISM

SEARCHING FOR PROFITS

The Portuguese, still trying to turn a profit from the colony, now turned to "chartered" companies. These companies were owned by large groups of businessmen who were given charters by the Portuguese government to develop land areas in Mozambique. As was often the case in colonial ventures, land that was "given" by a European power was already occupied by African people. For the Portuguese, it was more a question of finding a method that worked after the failure of the prazeiro system. The African people were not consulted or even considered in this plan. Many African people do not share the modern concept of private land ownership. They believe it is there to be used by all the people. Land isn't bought and sold. These ideas made them easy targets for the Portuguese.

Of the three companies that were chartered, the Zambézia Company was able to make a profit through its agricultural and mineral land rights. The second firm, The Mozambique Company, was heavily financed by British investors. It was granted control of the regions today known as Sofala and Manica Provinces. It was supposed to build all the facilities needed by a modern society: roads, ports, schools, and hospitals. It actually built only those facilities it needed for its own business.

FORCED LABOR

Although slavery had been outlawed, the Portuguese businessmen still depended on cheap or free labor, and they found ways around any law that was passed to protect the Africans. The Native Labor Code of 1878 was written to allow the Africans to choose whether they wanted to work for Europeans. At the same time, there was another law that anyone who was judged to be a vagrant—a person without financial support— could be forced to work. The Portuguese interpreted vagrancy as including anyone who chose to support himself by "traditional" work such as growing his own food, which meant that virtually everyone could be forced to work for the Europeans.

The Portuguese prevented African men from traveling to South Africa to work on plantations or in the mines, then forced them to work in Mozambique. They forced women to grow crops for sale to the company instead of being free to grow food for their own use. And finally, they established the "hut tax," a way of forcing people to earn money to pay to be allowed to live in their own houses. Forced labor instituted by the chartered companies became the rule in Mozambique and remained in effect well into the twentieth century.

The third group, the Nyassa Company, was responsible for destroying much of the family life in its designated region, the extreme north of Mozambique. The company was unable or unwilling to develop the land it was granted. Instead, the people in the area it controlled were sold as labor. The company's control was so brutal that many Africans ran away to neighboring territories that were ruled by Germany and Britain. The result was a tremendous loss of population in the northern region of the territory.

LOCAL COLONIALISM

In 1907 Portugal moved the administration of the Mozambique colony from Lisbon, the capital of Portugal, to the district offices in Mozambique. Many of the district officials were poorly educated and often used physical violence to enforce the law. Corrupt district officials often kept much of the revenue their regions produced instead of sending it to the government in Portugal.

WORLD WAR I

Though it was located far from Europe, Mozambique was caught up in World War I along with Portugal. Hoping to protect its African colonies against a German victory, Portugal sided with the Allies. Thousands of Mozambican men were recruited, many by force, to fight against the Germans in nearby German East Africa. In 1917 there was a violent uprising against this policy. The Portuguese found themselves fighting both the Germans and the Africans in Mozambique. Ultimately, more than 130,000 Africans died as a result of the war, including soldiers as well as laborers pressed into the war effort. The Africans were spared the

*António Salazar, prime
minister of Portugal*

same fate during World War II, when Portugal remained neutral
and did not draw its colonies into the war.

NEW REGIME IN PORTUGAL

From 1932 until 1968, António Salazar was prime minister of
Portugal. Earlier he had been Portugal's finance minister and had
overhauled the colonial policy in an effort to make the colonies
more productive. Most of the Portuguese in Mozambique were
government officials, but by the 1950s a growing number of
Portuguese farmers had been settled in southern Mozambique.
They were part of another government plan to increase the white
Portuguese population in Mozambique, which by this time
numbered about fifty thousand.

BECOMING "CIVILIZED"

The Portuguese were convinced that they could turn Mozambique and their other African colonies into distant parts of Portugal. To make this come true, the Mozambicans would have to agree to become "civilized," according to Portuguese standards. The person had to speak Portuguese, had to give up his traditional culture, and had to be employed in business or industry. Anyone who met this test could apply to become an *assimilado*, an assimilated person. This person then was considered to be a Portuguese citizen, no longer subject to the rules applied to other Africans. The rest of the Africans—the vast majority— were called *indigenas*, "indigenous people," or the people of the land, and were judged according to different laws.

DRIVING PEOPLE AWAY

The real treatment of Africans in Mozambique continued to be so devastating under Salazar, however, that there was a steady flow of people out of Mozambique to neighboring countries. The secret police, PIDE, greatly feared in Portugal, were brought in to tighten Portuguese control in Mozambique. There were few options for Africans in Mozambique, especially in the area of employment. One of the few ways out was to accept contract labor in South Africa and work on a temporary but regular basis. Another was to find a permanent job in a neighboring territory and leave Mozambique entirely. By the 1950s some 500,000 Africans had left to find a better, safer place to live and work. Those who stayed behind were likely to end up working for nothing on public works projects.

*Migrant workers
leave Mozambique
heading for the
mines in South Africa.*

GOING TO THE MINES

The Portuguese always had regarded Mozambique and its
people as work units, to be used in any way that would profit
their country. Portugal even changed its policy of not allowing
men to work outside Mozambique when the Portuguese saw how
much they could benefit from taxing the men who went to work
in South Africa. This resulted in the destructive system known as
migratory labor. Men were needed in South Africa to work on the
sugar plantations, in the diamond fields, and in the gold mines.
The migrant workers left behind their families, their language,
and their culture. During the century of going to the mines, these
changes became a basic fact of Mozambique life and culture in the
rural areas where the only work available was farming.

Some of the men who left home to work in the mines were
trying to raise money to pay the bride price. Also known as

The Kimberly diamond mine

lobolo, or bride wealth, the money was paid to the bride's family as compensation because the family was losing a hard worker. Bride price was expensive and was traditionally paid in the form of hoes, farming implements. The marriage hoe, called a *beja,* was not made to be used. It was carefully kept and passed along to the next generation, when it would be used as bride wealth once again. It took cash to buy the beja, which was not made by blacksmiths. A typical bride price might be ten to fifteen hoes. To earn money for hoes and all the new family's household goods, men had to look for jobs outside Mozambique.

WORKING THE KIMBERLEY MINE

Men who traveled as far as Kimberley, the great diamond mine in the center of South Africa, tended to stay away for long

*The men worked hard in the mines (left) and
competed in dance contests (right) as a form of recreation.*

periods of time. They lived in hostels, large rooms like
dormitories, with many beds. This was different from life at
home. Mine work was not only strenuous, it was much more
dangerous than agricultural work because it involved the use of
machinery to a much greater extent. It was hard work in a much
colder climate than the men were used to, but it paid better than
plantation work.

A new, urban black culture began to develop around Kimberley,
and this development continued as the mine grew larger and
required the labor of thousands of men. Drinking alcohol with
their fellow workers became a social activity of its own in this
new kind of world. The men also competed in dance contests,
each group doing its own traditional dances. Dance contests
became a regular feature of life at the mines.

By the late 1880s the men were taking longer work contracts and spending longer periods, up to eighteen months, away from their families. This put a great strain on the women, who had to take over the roles traditionally played by men in addition to their own heavy workloads.

GOLD IS DISCOVERED

The demand for migrant labor skyrocketed after 1886 when gold was discovered in the area of South Africa called the Witwatersrand. By 1892 there were more than twenty-five thousand black workers in the gold fields. To control the flow of laborers from Mozambique, the Chamber of Mines in South Africa appealed to the Portuguese for help. The Portuguese earned a "passport" fee from each worker who left Mozambique. At the gold mines, the Mozambicans worked together as a group. They became drilling specialists who worked at the "face" of the mine, the exposed rock where the gold was found in a "seam."

PORTUGUESE CONTROL MINE WORKERS

By 1895 the Portuguese had gained control over the southern part of Mozambique and were able to restrict the movement of the miners from the region. By 1909 the Portuguese had made a deal to exchange the labor of black Mozambican miners for the right to transport goods from the Transvaal Province of South Africa. The Portuguese established a policy of demanding payment in gold for the labor of the workers. They, in turn, paid the black workers in Mozambican currency. This policy continued throughout the colonial period, and after 1968 it became even more profitable for the Portuguese. At that time, although the price of gold on the world market started to rise, South African gold continued to be valued at the official price set by the Mozambican colonial authorities. They still paid the workers in local currency at the lower, official rate. Then they sold the gold in the world market and received tremendous profits. The workers had no way to benefit from this. Even for a few years after independence, this policy remained in effect.

It wasn't until 1978 that the arrangement was changed and the workers began to receive their wages at the better rate. By that time, however, the number of Mozambican workers being recruited to work in the mines had been reduced. In 1975, 118,000 men, mostly from the south of Mozambique, went to the mines. But in the years from 1977 to 1982, only about 41,000 to 46,000 men were hired each year. This hurt the mine workers directly and it also hurt Mozambique, which depended on the income from those workers.

When it became harder to find mine work, many people traveled over the border illegally to work on farms and in households in South Africa. About 40,000 Mozambicans are working in the South African mines again, but there are many thousands more looking for work. As many as 250,000 people slip over the border each year, illegally, with as many as 1 million already in the country. Those who are caught are sent back to Mozambique. But they will continue to migrate illegally as long as there is little work available in Mozambique. South Africans see these illegals as taking away the jobs needed for millions of their own people. With Mozambicans making up an estimated 70 percent of all illegal immigrants in South Africa, they have become a serious issue for the South African government.

Chapter 4

THE ROAD TO INDEPENDENCE

THE RISE OF NATIONALISM

In 1968 Marcelo Caetano replaced Salazar as prime minister of Portugal. Caetano was considered more moderate. By this time, pressure was being felt throughout Africa for independence from colonial powers. Under Caetano, Portugal made some changes in the way the Africans were governed, but it was too little, too late. The drive to be independent was sweeping the continent, and Mozambique was a part of that movement.

Several groups of Mozambicans threatened the continuation of the colonial system. Educated *expatriates*, people who had left Mozambique to live in other African or European countries, had grown into a considerable force. They began to organize politically and quickly realized that only independence from Portugal would enable them to take control of their own lives and live as first-class citizens.

Left to right: Marcelo Caetano, Julius Nyerere, and Eduardo Mondlane

HELPFUL NEIGHBORS

It was not possible for Africans to meet and make plans in Mozambique without drawing the attention of the secret police. They set up their offices in the neighboring countries of Rhodesia (now Zimbabwe), which still was fighting its own battle for independence, and newly independent Tanzania. Many Mozambican leaders were living in Tanzania and Kenya. They learned about political organization by helping those countries gain their independence.

In Tanzania, with the active support of its president Julius Nyerere, the representatives of three Mozambican liberation groups met in 1962. They agreed to merge into one new organization, known in Portuguese as *Frente de Libertação de Moçambique* (Frelimo). In English the name means "Front for the Liberation of Mozambique." Its leader, Eduardo Mondlane, had been educated in South Africa and abroad and had worked at the United Nations (UN) in New York. He set up Frelimo's headquarters in Dar es Salaam, the capital of Tanzania.

WAR FOR INDEPENDENCE

Mondlane and the other activists working to free themselves from Portuguese rule knew they faced a dangerous task. The Portuguese were fighting against a similar drive for independence in Angola. The Mozambicans knew that Portugal had responded with great force in Angola and that would be the case in Mozambique as well.

As Frelimo trained for armed resistance in camps in Tanzania, the Portuguese moved troops into Mozambique. By the time Frelimo made its first attacks in September 1964, the Portuguese had thirty thousand men in Mozambique. The Portuguese essentially gave up the northernmost provinces of Mozambique by declaring the region a "no-man's-land," a place that was off-limits to everyone. They pushed the local people southward into *aldeamentos,* fortified villages, meant in part to protect the people, but also to keep them out of reach of Frelimo. They knew Frelimo would be counting on the villagers for food.

At this time, the Portuguese made a belated attempt to win the support of black Africans. They began to offer basic education services as well as economic assistance, after decades of neglecting these needs.

Frelimo drew its strength in numbers from the north, especially among the Makonde people who lived along Mozambique's northern border. Although most of the guerrilla fighters came from the north, most of Frelimo's leaders, including Samora Machel, came from the south.

Ethnic differences as well as conflicting political ideas made it difficult for Frelimo to maintain a united front. These differences led to violent attacks within the group. Key Frelimo leaders were

Samora Machel (left), Frelimo's president, at first tried
to disrupt the construction of Cabora Bassa Dam (right).

killed in the late 1960s, including Mondlane, who died at
Frelimo's headquarters in Dar es Salaam when he opened a mail
bomb addressed to him. The Portuguese secret police were
actually responsible for many of these assassinations as they tried
to stop the liberation groups from succeeding.

Frelimo was receiving help from many different sources
including other African countries as well as countries in Europe
and Asia. Some gave weapons, some offered education and
scholarships, some helped with money, and others provided
military training.

MILITARY ATTACKS INCREASE

After Mondlane was assassinated, Samora Machel was named
Frelimo's president. With Machel in place, Frelimo increased its
military operations, focusing on the Tete District. They chose this
region in the central part of the country to halt, or at least
disrupt, Cabora Bassa, a huge hydroelectric project that Portugal
was trying to create in the Zambezi River valley.

The dam and energy plant had been under consideration for some time, but Portugal had been unable to fund it and, until 1962, had not allowed foreign investment in Mozambique. The dam was meant to supply energy to South Africa. The money earned would help develop Mozambique. Although Frelimo opposed the dam at first, in time it realized that the dam would be one of the few useful assets in Mozambique after independence.

WAR SPREADS

In the early 1970s the war in Mozambique spread. There were by now ten thousand Frelimo fighters. In response, the Portuguese added another sixty thousand troops, two-thirds of them black Africans. But no matter how many soldiers the Portuguese could command, they were faced with an enemy spread out over a huge portion of the country, an estimated 154,000 square miles (398,860 square kilometers).

PEACEFUL REVOLT IN PORTUGAL

Meanwhile, discontent was growing in Portugal itself over the cost to the country both in money as well as in soldiers' lives lost in these unpopular wars. These wars fought over distant lands meant little to the Portuguese people. They could see no benefit in losing their sons to keep control of the African colonies.

The real opening for independence for Mozambique came on April 25, 1974, when the Portuguese officers belonging to the Armed Forces Movement in Portugal staged a peaceful revolution. They threw out the government in power and set the stage for withdrawal of troops from Mozambique. But when they offered Frelimo the chance to take part in a democratic political process with other groups that had formed in Mozambique, Frelimo refused. Frelimo felt it had been responsible for forcing the Portuguese out. It demanded independence, with Frelimo established as the new government of Mozambique. The Portuguese leaders, knowing that Frelimo had no political representation in two-thirds of Mozambique, refused these demands and ordered the soldiers to continue to fight. But the cause was lost.

A few months later, despite opposition from other liberation groups based in southern and central Mozambique, the Portuguese gave in to Frelimo's demands. Frelimo was declared the sole representative of the Mozambique people. Samora Machel, representing Mozambique, and Mario Soares, Portugal's prime minister, agreed that Mozambique would become independent on June 25, 1975. The date was chosen because it was the anniversary of the founding of Frelimo in 1962. Joaquim Chissano, one of Frelimo's leaders, became the interim president during the transitional period leading up to independence.

OPPOSITION TO FRELIMO

But promises of independence and an end to the fighting did not end Mozambique's problems. Many groups were opposed to Samora Machel, who took over as president on June 25, 1975. Prominent among them were Portuguese whites, who were afraid of losing their farms in Mozambique. Former Frelimo members who had been forced out of the movement also opposed Machel.

In September 1974 before Frelimo took over the government of

Just before Mozambique gained independence, many Portuguese left the country.

Mozambique, the Portuguese radio station in Maputo was invaded by opponents of Machel. They began calling on the people of Mozambique to revolt against Frelimo. Guarded by former Portuguese soldiers, they broadcast a steady call to fight against Frelimo, which was to be installed as the new government later that month. Financial backing for the opposition movement came from a Portuguese businessman, millionaire Jorge Jardim.

From this radio station takeover, the idea of creating a group in opposition to Frelimo was born. This was the Mozambican National Resistance, better known as Renamo, the abbreviation for its Portuguese name. It was created in neighboring Rhodesia, still ruled by a white-minority government that feared Frelimo's control. With its help, Afonso Dhlakama, a black Mozambican, became head of Renamo.

WHITES FLEE MOZAMBIQUE

As soon as the collapse of the old Portuguese regime took place, great numbers of white farmers left Mozambique. Their

Portuguese returning to Portugal wait in Angola for transport.

farms had been the principal source of fresh vegetables as well as dairy and meat products for Mozambique's cities. They grew most of the country's export crops as well. Mozambique's whites continued to leave through the first six months of 1975, getting out before independence. The loss of all this skilled manpower was a tremendous blow to Mozambique's economic future.

By independence, an estimated 40,000 whites remained, down from 200,000. While some went back to Portugal, many moved a short distance away to South Africa. They thought that Renamo, partly supported by their funds, would be successful in taking over the government. Then they would return to Mozambique and what they considered a more favorable leadership. The number of whites continued to decline, and by 1977 there were only about 30,000 whites in the country, many of them foreign workers brought in on contracts to do the specialized jobs few Mozambicans had been trained to do.

Chapter 5

CREATING

A NEW COUNTRY

ESTABLISHING SOCIALIST RULE

When Samora Machel took over as president, he was
determined to overturn the country's economic structure, which
had benefited a few whites while using the labor of the blacks.
His first moves confirmed the whites' fears—he nationalized all
the land in the country. No individual was allowed to own land,
not even the land on which his house stood. Doctors and lawyers
were not allowed to have private clients. The missionary schools
were taken over by the government. Religious activities were
strongly discouraged.

Once independence was achieved and Machel was in power, he
made it difficult for most people to have any voice in the new
government. There was only one political party allowed—Frelimo.
Machel patterned the government of the country on that of the
Soviet Communist system (which no longer exists today), with all
decisions made by centralized committees. These policies were not
suitable for Mozambique, especially regarding agriculture, the
heart of its economy. In addition, Frelimo began restricting the
rights of the citizens and imprisoned thousands of people, often
with no proof of any wrongdoing.

Samora Machel became president of Mozambique in 1975.

OPPOSITION CONTINUES

Just at the time that Rhodesia was to become the independent nation of Zimbabwe in April 1980, Renamo's leaders were flown to a military base in South Africa where they continued to plan the fight against Frelimo.

By this time Samora Machel began to understand that his policies had caused major problems for the people in Mozambique. He started to change his policies so people could farm their own lands, rather than being forced to work on government collective farms. And he permitted the people to elect their own headmen or chiefs. But Machel found it hard to change. When the people chose the very chiefs that Machel had forced out of power when he became president, he refused to accept the results. He did not seem capable of understanding what the people wanted and needed. He preferred a model for governing that he had learned from the Chinese Communists, who had

47

supported him during his time in exile. Like the Chinese, Machel put a great deal of energy and money into literacy classes for the more than 90 percent of the peasants who could not read and write. But in their daily lives, this was not the most important thing. The people were used to getting the information that guided their lives from their chiefs and the elders of their communities.

NKOMATI ACCORD

The Mozambique government knew that the government of South Africa was involved in financing and supporting Renamo, in addition to the money coming from the white Mozambicans living in South Africa. The South African government knew that Mozambique was supporting the African National Congress (ANC), the group fighting to end *apartheid* (racial segregation) and bring democracy to South Africa. Machel was so desperate to stop Renamo, which he felt was destroying Mozambique, that he signed an agreement with South Africa. It was called the Nkomati Accord, named for the river at the border town of Komatipoort, where Machel met the South African representative. Machel agreed to end support for ANC bases in Mozambique, and P.W. Botha, president of South Africa, agreed to stop supporting Renamo. But as the war continued it became obvious that only the Mozambicans were keeping up their end of the deal.

By 1985 Renamo had grown strong and was well established in Mozambique's provinces. A drought that had plagued the region in the early 1980s also played a role in convincing the people that supporting Renamo offered them a better future than they would have with the Frelimo government.

This house in Gaza Province was destroyed by Renamo forces.

Many of the people most severely affected by the drought had been forced to abandon their farms. Most of the areas worst hit by the drought were in the midsections of the country, on both sides of the Zambezi River. Because Renamo was strong in this region, there was a fear that Mozambique itself would be divided in half.

As the war continued, the Frelimo government was reduced to running the cities and towns. It could not guarantee any kind of aid or food to the people in the countryside where Renamo was destroying the lives of the peasants.

Renamo was intent on destroying every building that Frelimo erected. Its only ideology was to destabilize the country so that it could not function. Renamo wanted to end Samora Machel's rule to create a capitalist government. Renamo's leader, Afonso Dhlakama, said, "No guerrilla movement has ever seized power without first battering its enemy to its economic knees." But Dhlakama went even further. He destroyed everything his men could reach: every little school and clinic in the countryside, water

People displaced by the war

systems, and other structures, no matter how small. Destroying
the physical structure was not all. A Renamo "signature" was to
cut off a person's ears or part of the nose as a warning to anyone
who might cooperate with the government.

Food supplies were virtually nonexistent. Stores in Maputo were
nearly empty, though Maputo had the best chance of receiving
supplies. There simply were no stores at all in the countryside.
Fuel supplies likewise were nearly used up. Most Mozambicans
were living on food donated by relief agencies.

By 1985 Renamo was attacking sites within thirty miles (forty-
eight kilometers) of the capital. Eight thousand soldiers from
Zimbabwe had been sent to guard the Beira Corridor, the
important transportation lines that stretched from the Zimbabwe
border to the port of Beira. The presence of the soldiers turned
the corridor into a kind of extended village. People came to live
near the railroad tracks and the road, feeling more secure there on
the cleared land than in the fields and forests.

Alberto Chissano

PRESIDENT MACHEL DIES

On October 19, 1986, Mozambican president Samora Machel was killed in a plane crash while returning home from a meeting with the presidents of Zambia, Angola, and Zaire. Joaquim Alberto Chissano was named president of Mozambique. He had been the country's foreign minister since independence in 1975 and represented a change of leadership attitudes. Unlike Machel, who had completed only four years of primary school education in Mozambique and was later trained as a nurse, Chissano was well educated. Although the tragedy of Machel's death was felt throughout Mozambique, Chissano probably was a more suitable leader to bring the country through the next years of war and to make peace with Renamo.

CHISSANO GETS HELP

In 1987 Chissano began receiving help in his fight against the rebels. Great Britain and other British Commonwealth nations offered military and economic assistance to protect railways, ports, and development projects against attacks by Renamo. Without this protection, anything built with outside help would become a new target for Renamo. Even so, in November 1988, Renamo blew up nine hundred of the four thousand pylons that carried electricity from the Cabora Bassa Dam. This brought to fourteen hundred the number of towers destroyed.

By 1989 the devastation of Mozambique seemed total, yet the war continued. More than 1.5 million people had fled the country, most of them reaching Malawi, others going into South Africa, Zimbabwe, and Swaziland. Four million others had simply abandoned their homes and farms and had sought shelter somewhere else within Mozambique. It is believed that as many as 1 million people had died, either by being caught in the warfare or from starvation.

However, remarkable changes were happening outside Africa, changes that would play an important role in Mozambique's future. In November 1989 the Berlin Wall fell, ending the division of Germany, followed by the collapse of the Soviet Union. The threat of Communist support for a black-ruled South Africa had virtually vanished. Now it would be much easier for the new South African president, F.W. de Klerk, to undertake his remarkable plan to end apartheid and make black majority rule possible. This meant the end of South African support for Renamo, since a black-ruled South Africa would not be sympathetic to the white Mozambicans.

Left: F.W. de Klerk, South Africa's president, ended apartheid in 1991. Right: President Chissano embraced the leader of Renamo, Afonso Dhlakama, after the peace treaty was signed.

PEACE ACCORDS SIGNED

Although cease-fire agreements were signed in 1990, it was not until October 4, 1992, that Renamo and Frelimo signed a peace agreement in Rome, Italy, officially ending the war in Mozambique. Crucial to this agreement was the demobilization of the country's two armies. Both sides were required to have their soldiers report to assembly points, with United Nations personnel overseeing the process. There were estimated to be twenty thousand Renamo and seventy thousand government troops. When they arrived in camps like the one in the city of Massingir, they were to turn in their weapons and await further orders. About fifteen thousand men from each side would form the new Mozambique army. It was crucial to the continuation of the peace process that these soldiers turn in their arms before the elections. Otherwise, it was feared that the country might have the same experience as another former Portuguese colony, Angola. There, the rebels refused to accept the results of the election and they resumed fighting. In Mozambique, the lesson of Angola is very much on people's minds.

LAND MINES REMAIN

Today, long after peace came to Mozambique, there remains a task of enormous proportions, one that will not be completed for years. During the course of the war, many land mines were planted in the ground by both sides. No one kept track of where they were put or how many there were. Soldiers as well as civilians were vulnerable to the land mines as they went about their daily life in the camps. One soldier touched off a land mine and blew off his leg, from the knee down.

It is estimated that as many as two million land mines were placed in Mozambique. As soon as the peace accords were signed, the UN, working with USAID and a Norwegian group, began training people in the dangerous business of locating land mines and then defusing them. The return of the refugees is tied to the success of this work, because they must have the freedom to move about their farmland without fear of setting off a land mine.

GENUINE RECONCILIATION

On September 4, 1993, a year after the peace accords were signed, Renamo leader Afonso Dhlakama agreed to turn over territory under his control. The government agreed to appoint three Renamo officials from each of the country's ten provinces.

The UN's special representative, Dr. Aldo Ajello, worked with representatives of both Frelimo and Renamo to establish assembly points for their soldiers. Then, the UN's cease-fire commission made sure that the soldiers came into the approved assembly areas on schedule and surrendered their weapons. A total of forty-nine assembly areas were required because these soldiers, some ninety thousand in all, were scattered all over the country. As the two forces were dismantled, fifteen thousand men were taken from each side to form the new Mozambican Defense Force. The remainder of the men were helped to return to civilian life, and at the same time they were provided with an income because of the great shortage of jobs in Mozambique.

For soldiers who fought such a bitter war, the amazing thing is how peaceably they came together in the assembly camps. There was a forgiveness that would not have seemed possible just a short time before. This was a crucial step in preparing the country for the return of the refugees, for planting crops, and for taking the first steps back from the devastation of the long, brutal war.

PRESIDENT CHISSANO

In 1986 Joaquim Alberto Chissano became president of Mozambique after the death of President Samora Machel. Chissano had been active in the government. He was instrumental in the independence movement, helping to establish Frelimo in Tanzania, and working with its leader, Dr. Eduardo Mondlane.

Chissano was born in Gaza Province where he went to primary school. He attended high school in Maputo and then traveled to Portugal to begin his university training. He left Portugal after one year and went to France where he continued his college education and first became active in the independence movement. He serves today as both president of Mozambique and leader of the Frelimo political party.

Above: During the civil war Mozambicans left the country and lived in neighboring countries. Below: The girl on the left was in a camp in Swaziland and the one on the right was in Zimbabwe.

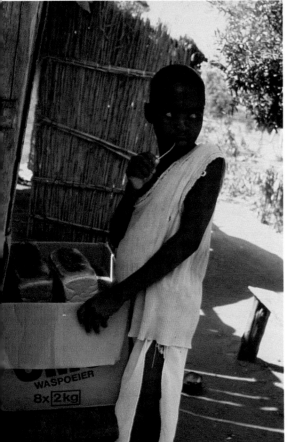

Chapter 6

REPATRIATION

MOZAMBICANS RETURN HOME

When war swept over Mozambique, the people fled in terror. With no way to know whether they would find safety or be refused entry, 1.6-1.7 million people ran from their homes and crossed the borders of Mozambique into foreign countries. Because Mozambique borders on six other nations, people wound up in different countries, depending on the part of Mozambique where they lived.

In Zambia, Zimbabwe, and Swaziland, the people were housed in refugee camps run by the United Nations High Commissioner for Refugees (UNHCR). In Malawi and South Africa they depended on the local people to assist them. By the time the war was over, 1 million people had poured over the border into Malawi. Malawi's president and its people accepted the refugees with remarkable generosity, even though some were forced to stay for as long as nine years.

Many aspects of this refugee situation were unique. Often when people flee their countries and stay in neighboring countries for long periods, they eventually become accepted in those countries and never go home. Sometimes they are even part of the same

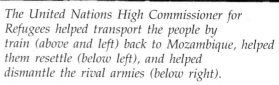

The United Nations High Commissioner for Refugees helped transport the people by train (above and left) back to Mozambique, helped them resettle (below left), and helped dismantle the rival armies (below right).

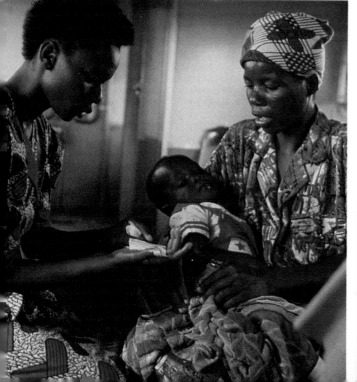

ethnic group in the new country and can blend in easily. But in the case of Mozambique, there was a strong push to get the refugees back home as soon as it was safe. Malawi has a limited amount of farmland, and nearly all the refugees were farmers. It also was important to bring home the important educated professionals whose skills were needed in Mozambique.

UNITED NATIONS IN MOZAMBIQUE

Never in the fifty-year history of the UN had so many demands been made for its help around the world. The role of the UN peacekeepers in Mozambique has been among the most successful in its history. Their major jobs were supervising the removal of land mines and assisting in the return of the refugees. It also was responsible for overseeing the dismantling of the two armies that fought in Mozambique. And it was given the task of monitoring the October 1994 elections to be sure they were free and fair.

The refugee repatriation program involved returning 1.6-1.7 million people to their homes from six neighboring countries. As part of that program, the UN helped rebuild water systems, roads, health clinics, and schools. Nearly eight thousand UN peacekeeping personnel were based in Mozambique.

The return of more than a million refugees from neighboring countries was accomplished slowly. Many people moved back on their own. For those who had lived in refugee camps organized by the UNHCR, the return was very organized. One such family included fifteen-year-old Cristina Mansuchal and her mother, brothers, sister, and grandmother.

The Mansuchal family lived in the UNHCR's Malindza refugee camp in Swaziland for five years. Cristina learned some English

Cristina (left) looks out the window of the train that is taking her home.
Cristina's brother played the guitar to entertain the travelers (right).

and continued her schooling, and the family had good medical care. Still they were all eager to get back to their home in Catembe, a village at the end of a peninsula across the bay from Maputo. Cristina and her family had learned that the war was over by listening to the radio, but they still had to wait until the peace agreement was signed before it was safe to go home.

Although they had left Catembe on foot and walked all the way to Swaziland, they returned on a refugee train organized by the International Organization for Migration (IOM). Each week, between seven hundred and one thousand refugees left this camp by train until the camp was empty and all the refugees were back in Mozambique.

The train ride home was exciting, but the sight of the devastation in Mozambique made the refugees aware of the huge job that awaited them. They not only had to rebuild their own homes and lives, but they now faced the tremendous task of rebuilding their country.

These youngsters, luckier than the street kids, are encouraged to draw and talk about their war experiences.

STREET CHILDREN

In Maputo many children, some as young as seven or eight, are roaming the streets. These are the street children, the ones who have no homes and who were separated from their families during the war. It is estimated that as many as a half million children are without their families. Some children earn a living on their own by selling small items to visitors and local people. Many of them do have parents but they don't know how to find them.

Among the many volunteer aid groups working with street children in the cities and with orphans in the countryside are Save the Children and the Institute for International Cooperation and Development (IICD). IICD brings young adult volunteers to countries such as Mozambique, where they work with the villagers to care for orphaned children and help them learn practical skills so they can support themselves. Much of the volunteers' work involves planting useful crops.

These young men are basket sellers in the Costa do Sol.

Because so much of village life was destroyed by the war, many of these children had no place to go to look for their families. They did not even know if their parents were alive, and parents did not know if their children were alive. A U.S.-based organization called Save the Children set about to try to reunite families that had been torn apart by the war.

Save the Children's most important weapon in this battle has been the camera. Photographs are taken of the children and then widely circulated in places where people might recognize them. As soon as someone recognizes one of the children, Save the Children then tries to match the child with a family member. Using a computer, the group has created a database of displaced children and their families. It can be difficult to make the match if the families have been separated a long time. Many of the children have been forced to kill people, to steal, and to live without thought for others. These children and young adults will have to start life all over again, hoping that they will not have to worry about the war anymore. But for the twenty thousand children that Save the Children has reunited with their families, at least they are back where they belong.

Chapter 7
PEOPLE AND CULTURE

THE ROLE OF LANGUAGE

More than sixty distinct ethnic groups make up the sixteen million plus people who live in Mozambique and speak their traditional language, the language of their culture, as well as Portuguese, the language they learn in school. The most widely used languages include Tsonga, spoken by about one-fourth of the people in Mozambique, and the group of languages known as Macua-Lomue, spoken by about one-third of the people. Tsonga and related languages are spoken in Maputo and by the mine workers who traveled to South Africa. Yao and Makonde are spoken in the country's far north. More than one-third of the people are Makua-Lomue. Most people who speak languages in this group live north of the Zambezi River.

All these languages also are spoken by many other people in neighboring countries. These language groups remind us that when the European powers drew boundaries to mark off their colonies, they didn't take into account the distribution of the African people. As a result, people speaking Makonde live on the border with Tanzania, and Tsonga-speaking people live in neighboring South Africa as well as in Mozambique. One of the largest language groups consists of the Shona/Shangaan speakers who live along the border with Zimbabwe. All of these cultural links allowed Mozambique refugees to find homes in neighboring countries where they spoke the same languages.

Along the northern part of Mozambique's coast, Swahili is widely spoken. Swahili was passed along by the traders who sailed the Indian Ocean. President Chissano speaks Swahili as well as several other languages.

Because Portuguese was the language used in schools and because the textbooks were in Portuguese, it has remained the language of the government and business. But Mozambique shares its borders with six countries where English is the language of government and business. Most tourists and businessmen coming to Mozambique are South Africans so English is being heard more often in Maputo.

Languages are lively things, and the more they are used, the more they tend to change. Tsonga words have made their way into the Portuguese language. English words are used all over the world, especially in the fields of science and computers, and these are making their mark as well.

HEALTH

Health conditions in Mozambique were dramatically affected by the movement of millions of people during the war. Some received good care at health clinics at refugee camps, whereas others had no access to medical care. At independence, or shortly

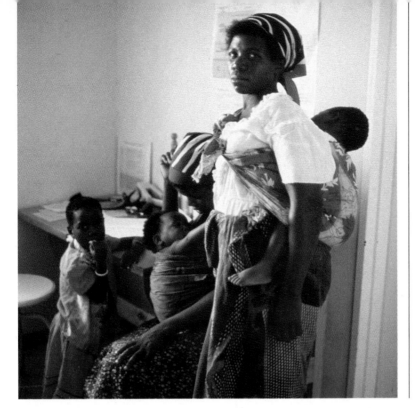

A Mozambican refugee woman takes her children to a medical clinic.

after, most of the country's 550 fully trained doctors left Mozambique because they were no longer allowed to have private practices. The government felt that well-qualified nurses could take care of much of the preventive medicine. The most important part of this care would be vaccinating children against contagious diseases, especially smallpox. Then by establishing clean water supplies and sanitation they hoped to reduce occurrence of diseases such as malaria and tuberculosis.

Most of the clinics that were established for this kind of health care were destroyed during the war. To get as many people as possible back under some kind of health-care program, the government put a great deal of money into rebuilding health-care facilities and training medical workers. It also overturned the law against private practice and hopes to entice doctors to return to Mozambique.

Mozambique is severely affected by two diseases carried by insects: sleeping sickness, carried by the tsetse fly, and malaria, transmitted by mosquitoes. Northern Mozambique is particularly affected by sleeping sickness. As for malaria, it is the most widespread disease in Africa. Researchers believe that about half the people of Africa carry the disease in their blood because they have been bitten by the malaria-carrying mosquito. Once someone has malaria, it remains in the system for life and attacks of extremely high fever can recur at any time. Malaria can cause death; about one million Africans die from the disease every year.

The most effective way to stop malaria is to eliminate mosquitoes. That is best done by draining swamps where mosquitoes like to breed.

RELIGION

The role of religion has frequently caused hostility, starting from the moment that Vasco de Gama made his way along the Mozambican coast in 1498. Vasco da Gama felt justified in firing on the Arab traders because they were Muslims. The Portuguese missionaries who made their way to Mozambique brought their own religion, Catholicism. They were followed by Protestant missionaries. Although these religions often were in conflict with the way people lived their lives, they offered something important —a chance to get an education. There was virtually no other way for an African in Mozambique to learn the basics of reading and writing—and to receive health care. The colonial Portuguese left the task of education to the Catholic mission schools because they didn't want to spend any money on educating the Africans.

In spite of this, most Mozambicans continued to follow traditional religious practices, and two-thirds of the people do so

Santo António da Polana Catholic Church

today. These beliefs help people to accept the events of their everyday life. They feel a close connection with their ancestors, as well as with the spirit world. They seek out traditional healers and spiritualists to cure illnesses, both physical and mental. The Western church missionaries who tried to convert Mozambicans to Western beliefs insisted that the native Africans forsake their traditional practices. But many of the people who are officially members of either a Christian or Islamic group also retain their traditional religious beliefs. An estimated 10 percent of the people are Muslims; about 20 to 30 percent identify themselves as Christians. When Mozambique became independent under Frelimo, the constitution specifically drew a line between religion and government. It also added that citizens were guaranteed the right "to practice a religion or not." The new government felt it necessary to say this because so much of the education of the people was being carried out by the churches.

Left: High school students concentrate on an examination.
Right: Children in a rural school

EDUCATION

People who were educated during the colonial era were taught in Portuguese and studied the same subjects as children living in Portugal, including Portuguese traditions. Exams were given about things that happened in Portugal; students knew about the geography of Europe but not about Africa. The first university in Mozambique opened in 1962 in Maputo, but only a handful of Africans were able to reach that level of education.

At independence, 90 percent of the people could not read or write. Only about five thousand black Mozambicans had more than four years of primary education. The new government set the task of giving all the people seven years of primary education, free of charge, although it was clear it would take a long time to train enough teachers and build enough schools to reach this goal.

An engineering student at the Naval School of Mozambique

The new government made a tremendous effort to bring some education to all Mozambicans. The number of children in primary school grew to more than one million just two years after independence. Literacy classes were offered for adults as well. Although there was a great push to make education equally available to both girls and boys, far fewer girls stayed in school after primary school. By that time, their parents preferred to keep them at home to help with farmwork, not seeing much benefit to be gained from further education.

Unfortunately, the war for control of an independent Mozambique put an end to many children's education. Schools were closed and often destroyed. Water and lack of food caused many to drop out. Even lack of clothing kept children at home.

A mural painted by Malangatana

CONTEMPORARY ART

Mozambique's cultural traditions extend to contemporary art. The most famous artist in Mozambique is Malangatana, whose outdoor murals are as well known to Mozambicans as some movie stars are to Americans. (Most Mozambican artists use only one name.) Malangatana paints the story of Mozambique, including the colonial period when he was growing up and the war. His paintings are crammed full of lively figures in a style that he created, but which is now widely copied. The most startling features are the white eyes looking out of black faces. These seem to leap out of his colorful canvases. One of Malangatana's most enthusiastic patrons is South African Albie Sachs, a supporter of Nelson Mandela and of the ANC's drive for black majority rule, who lived in exile in Mozambique for eleven

Left: Albie Sachs with Malangatana and one of his paintings
Right: Carving wood figures is an important and well-known craft.

years. During that time he bought many of Malangatana's paintings and murals and has now donated them to the Mayibuye Center at the University of the Western Cape in South Africa.

Sculpture is perhaps the most traditional kind of art created in Mozambique. The most familiar pieces are created by the Makonde people who live in the far north. Their complex "family tree" pieces tell stories through the expressions of the many figures carved from single pieces of ebony wood. One of the best-known Makonde sculptors is Nkatunga, who depicts daily life in the rural community.

There are other sculptors besides the Makonde. Chissano is a sculptor who expresses himself in wood, just as Malangatana did in painting. Chissano's work also tells the history of Mozambique. His pieces depict the struggles of the country through human figures. Although the works of both Chissano and Malangatana feature realistic images, some artists work in abstract images.

Boxes and baskets are made from reeds and ceramic vases (inset) are decorated with paper and then glazed.

CRAFTS FOR EVERY DAY

Beautiful images and ideas are expressed in the items that people make for daily use. These include baskets, mats, pestles to grind meal, handles for axes and hoes, and all kinds of cooking equipment. Working with available materials, including wood, cane, sisal, and shells, people make these practical items and then decorate them for the pleasure of having something beautiful in their hands every day.

Among the most admired crafts from Mozambique are the tapestries made in the province of Zambézia and shell ornaments made on Mozambique Island in Nampula Province.

Musicians in performance

MUSIC AND DANCE

Traditional music in Mozambique is performed on instruments made by the musicians for their own use. They make drums from wood, and the drumheads consist of stretched pieces of animal skins. Wind instruments, called *lupembe* by the Makonde, are traditionally made either from animal horns or from wood or gourds. *Marimbas*, also known as xylophones, are popular with the Chope musicians of southern Mozambique.

In the cities, a new kind of music has grown out of the traditions. It's called *marrabenta* and is based on traditional complex African rhythms. American jazz also was greatly influenced by African rhythms.

Dance is so much a part of traditional life that when Mozambican men went to the gold mines to work, dancing on Sunday was their principal entertainment. In rural areas, dancing is a form of communication and expression. Only after independence were the African dances of Mozambique considered to have value. Missionaries often frowned on ethnic dances, finding them too full of passion and excitement. Now the people can celebrate their most important dances, including the *mapiko* from Cabo Delgado in the north, the *tufo* of Mozambique Island, the *nhau* from Tete Province, and the *chingomana,* popular in Gaza, Inhambane, and Maputo Provinces.

PRESERVING CULTURE

There is a national dance company in Mozambique that travels around the country presenting authentic dance performances and helping to save the culture.

An organization called Nambu Productions promotes contemporary art based on the traditional culture of Mozambique. It organizes exhibitions of Mozambican sculpture and other work and also helps promote Mozambican folk songs and dance by staging demonstrations for tourists who visit the main towns.

The director of tourism, António Yok Chan, says, "It is important to preserve the cultural identity and features of each region."

STORYTELLERS

In many African societies that have no written language, the elders keep the knowledge and wisdom of their people and pass it along by telling their people's stories over and over. This is known as an oral tradition.

Stories and proverbs, myths, and jokes, all part of Mozambique's oral tradition, were told aloud and passed along in this way from generation to generation. They were not written down. Although the idea of written stories began more recently, Mozambique has a wealth of fine writers. They wrote during the colonial period when much of their work was censored by the Portuguese. Out of this struggle emerged poets and novelists, some of them gaining worldwide attention. One of the best known is Mia Couto, who published his first poem in a local newspaper when he was fourteen years old. His novels include *Sleepwalking Land* and *Voices Made Night*. He is known for his great imagination, and for coining new phrases to express his ideas. He has been called "Dreamer of Memories."

Many writers struggle for literary recognition. Writer Luis Bernardo Honwana fought for the independence of Mozambique and was imprisoned for his efforts. His talents as a writer and as a documentary filmmaker have earned him awards and the title of minister of culture. Using the background of his own life, Honwana's stories tell the struggle of his people. His best-known book is *We Killed Mangy-Dog*.

Poet José Craveirinha has been one of the most vigorous defenders of the continuing use of Portuguese as the official language in Mozambique. Even so, he doesn't mind the introduction of foreign words into the language, including words from local African languages. He has seen that words created in Mozambique have made their way to Brazil and other Portuguese-speaking countries. In one of his poems, "The Seed is in Me," he writes about the "mingling in his veins," a reference to the mixing of African and Portuguese ancestry. Another author, Noémia De Sousa, has been called the "mother" of the Mozambican writers. When she was writing in the 1950s and 1960s, she was the only mestiça writing in Portuguese in Africa. Her subject was all around

Maria Mutola runs the 800-meter race.

her—the women who were overburdened with children and work. Among her poems is "If You Want to Know Me" in which she writes about a Makonde carver creating a carved figure: "Africa from head to toe,—ah, she is who I am!"

SPORTS

While few people have been able to follow or enjoy sports because of the long war, they remain great sports fans, especially of soccer. But while Mozambique does not yet field a world-class soccer team, it does have some of the best runners in the world. The best-known runner in Mozambique, and easily the most recognized woman in the country, is Maria Mutola. She played soccer as a girl and competed against boys throughout her early years, but when she reached 18, she was rejected by the soccer federation because she was a woman. She turned to running and, to her amazement, quickly became the best in the world in her event, the women's 800-meter race. She won a gold medal at the world championship and plans to compete in the Olympic Games in Atlanta, Georgia, in 1996. She was presented a special gold medal by President Chissano for her achievements.

Chapter 8

A NATION OF FARMERS

AGRICULTURE

Most of the people of Mozambique are farmers who depend on the land for their food and their living. They must work hard to produce crops because the land in Mozambique is not particularly rich farmland, and sometimes there is not enough rainfall for the crops. Often the people cannot grow enough food and they have to rely on imported grain. While the land is not the best for farming, there is quite a lot of it.

Farming methods for most of the people are very basic. They work the land by hand, with few tools, and count themselves lucky if they have oxen to help with the labor.

CASH CROPS

During the colonial period, many peasant farmers were forced to grow cotton and other crops that could be sold for cash by the Portuguese. Workers were forced into the labor system called *shibalo*, which means "serf" in the Swahili language. The system was especially severe in northern Mozambique, resulting in great shortages of food. Farmers who refused to participate were

Farm women bring their vegetables to market (left).
Workers line up to have their baskets of tea weighed (right).

severely punished. Whereas the African farmers were forced to work for the Portuguese, white settlers from Portugal were given large areas of land and cheap loans to prepare the land for agriculture.

CASHEW NUTS

Many farmers harvested cashew nuts from trees that were brought to Mozambique from Brazil by Portuguese missionaries in the sixteenth century. The farmers took the nuts from the millions of wild trees. They were not willing to plant trees that take as long as twelve years before they produce full crops. At one time, Mozambique was the world's largest supplier of these tasty nuts. Other crops include sisal, sugarcane, and tea. For local use, farmers grow cassava, maize, millet, rice, and sorghum, as well as some fruits and potatoes. Many foods and plants we think of as typically African, such as cassava, were not native to that continent.

Cashew nuts are cleaned and sorted.

Cashew nuts became a cash crop in the 1920s and continued to be the country's most important source of foreign exchange or hard currency. When a country has a weak currency, or one that is not accepted in any other country, it must earn foreign currency. The way to do that is to sell its products or crops outside the country.

The cashew crop reached a high of 216,000 tons (196,000 metric tons) in 1972, when Mozambique was the biggest producer in the world. When manufactured goods stopped coming into the country because of the new government's policies, farmers found they had no use for the cash they earned and they stopped collecting the nuts. By 1982 production fell to a low of 18,000 tons (16,000 metric tons). It began to rise again in 1992 and is on its way up. Cashew nuts are a perfect crop for small-scale farmers, and they find a ready market abroad.

OTHER CASH CROPS

Sugarcane, the source of sugar, was the second most important crop in Mozambique both before and after independence. But by the 1980s production of sugar had dropped. Sugarcane harvesting requires hand labor, which was supplied by force during the colonial period. Tea, another important crop, continued to be grown through the early 1980s. Most of the plantations are located in Zambézia Province. Cotton grown by forced labor in Mozambique was intended for Portugal's textile industry to help Portugal compete against its more-advanced European competitors. Like the other labor-intensive crops, cotton production dropped considerably. One of the problems was the lack of mechanical harvesters suitable for use on large farms. Now cotton production is coming back thanks to a major investment by Lonrho, a British-based company that is one of the biggest investors in agriculture and mining in Africa.

At Chokwe Estate, located near the Limpopo River, an irrigation system was created in the 1950s. This system is still in place and can be used to supplement natural rainfall.

BACK TO THE LAND

When the war engulfed Mozambique, the people fled their farms. In addition to more than 1.6 million people who wound up in Malawi, Zimbabwe, South Africa, and Swaziland, about 4 million others were forced off their lands and lived out the civil war years in squatter camps near the cities within Mozambique.

By the time of the October 1994 elections, these people had

been moved back onto the land. Most of them were left without seeds or even the simplest farm tools to work the land. They had to rely on donations from many countries to get started again. When the people moved back, they arrived just before the rainy season began so they had a chance of planting their crops.

While they wait for the crops to grow, they will use food donated by the relief agencies. They can count on receiving food for one year. By then they will have gotten their own farms going and have stored up enough food to see them through until the next harvest.

As soon as people start producing grain and have more than they need for their own use, the World Food Program buys it and distributes it in other areas of the country. This gives the farmers an "instant" market for their crops and encourages them to plant more. There are many volunteers in Mozambique who are helping people get more out of their farms and are introducing new crops, including vegetables, that will vary diets and give people better nutrition. They also show how crop rotation can help improve the soil. Farmers are growing rice as well as traditional African grains.

FISHING

With the long coastline, fishing always has been a way of life for many Mozambicans. Independent fishers or small commercial businesses were the rule, with the rich waters providing tons of fish and shrimp. Foreign boats, with their mechanized methods, were kept out of the region until the mid-1960s. Portuguese commercial fishers were active in Mozambique before independence. When Frelimo came to power, these fishers

*Fresh shrimp, which have been caught in nets (right),
are grilled and served with lime (left).*

abandoned their equipment, which was taken over by the
government. By the early 1980s, fishing accounted for nearly 20
percent of all export income.

Mackerel, anchovies, and prawns (shrimp) are the principal
products of Mozambique's fisheries. In addition to ocean fishing,
Mozambique's sixty rivers also provide good fishing in many
parts of the country.

BUSINESS AND INDUSTRY

As soon as the peace accords were signed on October 4, 1992,
the Mozambican economy began to revive. By 1993 the country
was already showing overall financial growth. Beira, Nacala, and
Maputo are important ports for products coming from Zimbabwe,
Malawi, Zambia, and South Africa. The income from transporting
those products is part of Mozambique's financial picture. As ports
and pipelines, roads and railroads are reconstructed and used by

These Mozambicans are employed in an orange juice factory (left) and a plastics factory (right).

neighboring countries, the economy should experience a tremendous boost. Taking advantage of the expertise available in the region, Mozambique has turned over the operation of some of the terminals at the ports to companies from South Africa and Zimbabwe.

Several hundred companies have been returned to private ownership after Samora Machel's nationalization was shown to be a failure. There are factories making textiles, some making plastics, and others processing oranges for juice and canning pineapples. Cashews are processed for overseas markets.

About half of the country is covered with forests and woodlands; this is unusual in Africa, where many areas have been stripped bare of wood for use as fuel. Some regions of Mozambique have lost many trees, especially where the refugees gathered near the borders. But Mozambique still has huge reserves of forestland that offer ample opportunity for logging, although conservationists are trying to establish sensible policies so the forests continue to renew themselves.

A street vendor opens a fresh coconut with a machete (left).
Watermelon is sold along the roadway (right).

Schools to train electricians and maritime schools to train seamen are turning out a new skilled workforce. Even the presence of street vendors offering cashews, coconuts, watermelon, and crafts shows how quickly a country at peace can start getting back on its feet.

MINERAL WEALTH

Although Mozambique's mineral resources have scarcely been developed, they should prove to be a good source of income as well as employment. There are enormous deposits of coal, beryllium, and limestone. Mozambique is thought to have the world's largest reserve of tantalite, a mineral used in producing electricity. There also are significant deposits of other minerals, including apatite, bauxite, fluorite, graphite, and magnetite. These mineral deposits are located in many different areas of the country and could offer employment for people in those areas. One mineral that has been mined quite extensively is coal,

Gold miners in South Africa

although during the war years production declined because the rail lines used to transport coal were attacked.

Other than the coal mines, most of the mines now in operation are quite small. However, Mozambican mining firms as well as those from South Africa already are looking into the tantalite deposit at Murrua. The beaches themselves are known to contain valuable minerals, especially along the coastline of Zambézia and Nampula Provinces. Graphite mining in Cabo Delgado Province is getting under way.

Mining offers Mozambique the best chance to quickly increase its exports. Because so many Mozambican men have had experience in the gold mines of South Africa, there is a large group of people who are already trained in mining techniques. They could play an important role in the future economy of the country.

Reserves of natural gas are found in great quantities in Inhambane Province. South Africa already has agreed to work with Mozambique to export gas through a long pipeline that also will serve the people in Maputo.

The Cabora Bassa Dam was completed in 1980.

MODERN UTILITIES

Although Mozambique does not have any known sources of oil that could be used for energy, it has many rivers. To create energy, rivers are dammed, creating large lakes behind the dams. When the water is released, it turns turbines that generate electricity. The electricity produced by these dams is carried many miles over wires supported by pylons to places where it will be used. The largest dam in Mozambique is Cabora Bassa on the Zambezi River. The dam took many years to build and was completed in 1980.

During the civil war many of these pylons were destroyed. Now, thanks to the cooperation of several countries in the region, the pylons are being rebuilt and the system reconnected. When the system is fully operational, much of the electricity will be

Pequenos Libombos Dam

consumed by South Africa, as originally planned. But there also will be lines to link the city of Maputo to the electrical grid, as well as neighboring Zimbabwe.

Mozambique will earn a good deal of money from the electricity it supplies to South Africa. The new government in South Africa has pledged to bring electricity to millions of black people for the first time; the Cabora Bassa electricity will help make that promise come true.

There also are many smaller dams on some other rivers in Mozambique. Often these were left unfinished because of the disruptions caused by the civil war. One recently completed dam is Pequenos Libombos. As they are completed, the dams will supply various regions of Mozambique with electricity. Without electrical power, farmers cannot use modern equipment, factories cannot be built or run, and the growth of the economy is limited.

Maputo, the capital city

★ Maputo

Chapter 9

MODERN MOZAMBIQUE

CITIES

Although Mozambique's people suffered through a long, destructive war, its cities were scarcely affected. The cities of Mozambique reflect the Portuguese colonial period more than other areas because most of the Europeans lived in the cities. Although the coastline is dotted with small settlements, the two principal cities of Maputo and Beira are the major population and business centers of the country.

MAPUTO

Until independence in 1975, Maputo was known as Lourenço Marques, named for the Portuguese explorer who first arrived here on his way to India. The city has been the capital of Mozambique since 1898, replacing Ilha de Moçambique, the first capital.

Maputo is the most populous city and has one of the best harbors along the country's long coastline. The harbor is well protected from the open sea by a peninsula of land that loops around the city. With its deepwater facilities, Maputo was an

Maputo harbor is protected from the open sea by a peninsula of land.

important outlet to the sea for Mozambique's landlocked neighbors. It was also an important port for South Africa because it was close to some of South Africa's manufacturing centers.

The first name of the city was *Baía da Lagoa,* which means "bay of the lagoon" in Portuguese. Three rivers make their way into the bay at this point.

Maputo is a major port, able to handle the largest freighters with modern cargo-hoisting devices. There was a cold-storage plant for fruit, a plant for freezing fish, and special equipment for handling sugar and grain shipments. During the war most of these facilities fell into disuse, but many are now being renovated.

Because Maputo is a hilly city, it has excellent viewing spots where large areas may be seen at a glance. From these places

Above: Maputo's beaches are known throughout southern Africa.
Below: A busy street with apartment buildings (left) and women
from Catembe carrying vegetables to sell in the market (right)

The luxurious Polana Hotel, with its outdoor pool (above), caters to a wealthy class of tourists (below).

The Maputo train station

visitors can spot the various museums, the main library, and the imposing city hall building, as well as the gardens that are scattered throughout the city. Although all the streets have names, they have not been repainted on the curbstones for twenty years and are invisible to anyone driving or walking around. The people who live in Maputo know where they are going, but it is very difficult for visitors. Landmarks such as the beautiful railroad station are sometimes the only way visitors can tell where they are.

The famous Polana Hotel, which was the center of fine dining and entertainment in Maputo, has been renovated. Its reopening was the signal of Mozambique's return to normal life. This elegant old hotel with its beautiful garden and swimming pool suffered mostly from neglect during the war.

New housing in Beira

BEIRA

Beira, Mozambique's second most important city, has a continental atmosphere similar to that of Maputo, with its Portuguese restaurants, bars, and entertainment. Fresh seafood and a refreshing ocean climate were greatly appreciated by visitors from landlocked Rhodesia. During the Portuguese colonial period, many apartment buildings were erected; these were virtually abandoned after the independent government of Mozambique made all buildings the property of the state. Now they are inhabited mostly by squatters who pushed into the cities to get away from the war in the countryside.

Although the port city of Beira does not have a naturally deep harbor, it was the main port for goods moving in and out of Zimbabwe, especially during that country's fight for

The port of Nacala has modern facilities.

independence, and the country of Malawi. Located several hundred miles up the coast from Maputo, Beira's harbor is quite shallow, and ships must enter the port through a long, narrow channel. Beira was designed to accommodate shipments of coal and to allow oil freighters to tie up and unload oil into a pipeline that reaches to the town of Mutare in Zimbabwe, a distance of 180 miles (290 kilometers). There is a rail line as well as a road extending across Mozambique from Zimbabwe to Beira, and this triple transportation link—railroad, road, and pipeline—became known as the Beira Corridor.

NACALA

Mozambique's third major port is Nacala, far to the north. Unlike the two other ports that developed in the late 1800s, along with the railroads, Nacala was built in the late 1960s. It has a fine, well-sheltered harbor that is naturally deep and able to accommodate large ships. Its modern facilities make it one of the highest-rated ports along the East African Coast. However, the deterioration of the railroad that leads from the port through the interior and to Malawi has caused use of the port to drop considerably.

RAIL TRANSPORTATION

Mozambique's rail system was devised during the colonial period and was built to serve the needs of the neighboring countries. It was built to transport minerals being mined in those countries, not as transport for Mozambique. Although Mozambique is a long, narrow country with a distinctive north-south shape, the rail lines run principally east to west, to South Africa, Zimbabwe, and Malawi. The three lines reach their eastern terminals at Mozambique's major port cities of Maputo, Beira, and Nacala.

The lines do not connect with each other anywhere in the country. The rail lines are a strong indication of the value the Mozambique colony had for Portugal. The Beira line, for example, was built in the 1890s to assist the settlers in neighboring southern Rhodesia and to bring out Rhodesian agricultural and mineral products. When war broke out, the lines were not maintained, and Malawi virtually lost its only outlet to the sea. A rail line running from Maputo to Johannesburg took the miners to work in South Africa and brought them home, weighed down with household goods, when they returned at the end of their

Railroad tracks and trains of the Beira line

contracts. This line, out of service during the war, has just resumed operations and is once again carrying passengers between Johannesburg and Maputo.

ROADS

Like the railroads, the road system was originally created to connect the major cities with neighboring countries. A coastal road runs along the length of Mozambique linking the cities, from Maputo in the south all the way through to Beira and Nacala and reaching Mocímboa da Praia in the extreme north. The interior of the country has few roads other than those created for the military during the 1960s. Many smaller roads are usable only during the dry season. In the rainy season, dirt roads that cover large parts of the country can be impassable. Because of the lack of a road network, the three main areas of the country remain isolated from one another. Two major road-building projects are well under way, improving the existing roads connecting Maputo with Ressano Garcia, a South African border town, and the town of Namaacha, and leading to the border town of Goba in Swaziland. This is the first time in twenty years that Swazis have enjoyed a short route to the beaches on the Mozambique coast. South Africans will benefit even more since they go to the coast in large numbers, driving through Swaziland on their way.

AIR TRANSPORT

In a country the size of Mozambique, with poor roads and few rail lines, it is natural that air transportation would be important. During the 1930s and up to the early 1950s, a luxury airliner called the "flying boat" carried people from Lisbon to Ilha de Moçambique. It was called a flying boat because of its great size and because it landed only on water. Such an aircraft did not need airstrips or airports, making it ideal for use in the coastal areas of Africa where it made stops. This service was the major lifeline for the colonials. Today Mozambique's state-owned airline, Linhas Aereas de Moçambique (LAM), offers international service to a few African and European capitals—Johannesburg, Harare, Paris, and London—as well as to major cities within the country. There were international airports in Maputo and Beira, now being restored, as well as more than twenty airfields in provincial capitals and the larger towns.

TOURISM

Before the war for independence and the civil war that followed, Mozambique was a favorite tourist destination. Many

A nightclub in Maputo

South Africans, as well as landlocked Rhodesians, considered the beach resorts to be an ideal honeymoon spot. They liked the bars and restaurants that stayed open till late at night, something they could not find in South Africa.

Since the end of the war and the return of visitors to Maputo, the restaurants and nightclubs have come to life again. After many years of silence, music can be heard late at night on Bagamayo Street, one of the liveliest in the city. The charming old buildings are being repainted and renovated, and Maputo is ready to reclaim its position as a tourist destination for all of southern Africa.

Vendors come to the area around the Polana Hotel in Maputo hoping to sell their wares to visitors. Goods are priced in foreign currency—American dollars and South African rands—it's all

Beaches stretch along
the Costa do Sol
for miles and miles.
Visitors can enjoy
volleyball, windsurfing,
or just relaxing.

welcome to these people who were unable to do any business throughout the long years of the war.

For people in Johannesburg, the beaches of Mozambique are closer than the nearest South African beaches in Durban and a great deal less crowded. The Costa do Sol, just a few miles from the center of Maputo, is the favored destination of beach goers. The beaches stretch for miles along the coast of the Indian Ocean. Offshore lie beautiful coral reefs teeming with exotic fish that easily can be explored with a snorkel and a pair of fins. Beachfront meals featuring lobster and the spicy dish known as prawns *piri-piri* can be found at restaurants and snack bars.

Mozambique is renowned for its sportfishing. Visitors can rent boats and fishing tackle for the day and fish for many deep-sea species including huge marlin, sailfish, swordfish, and hammerhead sharks. Swordfish can weigh as much as 175 pounds (79 kilograms), and a marlin that weighed 750 pounds (340 kilograms) was caught off Bazaruto. The local maritime club runs contests for fishers with trophies and cash prizes awarded for the biggest fish caught.

Five islands off the Mozambique coast form the Bazaruto Archipelago. Islands in this group range in size from the largest, Bazaruto, twenty-six miles (forty-two kilometers) long and about twenty-four miles (thirty-nine kilometers) wide, to the smallest, Bangue, not big enough to have any permanent inhabitants. The islands have been designated as a national park, balancing the needs of the people who live there with those of the tourists, who can bring in welcome income.

A limited number of visitors can travel to the coral reef islands of Margaruque, Benguerra, and Bazaruto by boat or seaplane.

These rarely visited islands have fine beaches and clear water for swimming and sunbathing. There are flamingos and dolphins and excellent bird-watching. The few thousand people who live on Bazaruto Island make their living from the sea catching parrot fish and turtles.

The Bazaruto Archipelago is a delicate environment, and it would be easy to overfish certain species. A local conservation project was established, with the help of the World Wide Fund for Nature, to work with the cooperation of the local fishers to set reasonable fishing quotas.

THE FUTURE OF WILDLIFE

The 5,000-square-mile (12,950-square-kilometer) Gorongosa Game Reserve, north of Beira, was the country's main game park before independence. In the days when hunting was allowed, it attracted twenty thousand tourists a year. They came to see its great herds of buffaloes, lions, elephants, hippos, and kudos. Then in 1973 the park was closed because of the war. In the late 1970s Renamo established one of its main bases of operation in the park and how much wildlife can be found there is a question.

Maputo Elephant Park, just south of the capital, once was a favorite place to see herds of elephants. Sadly, visitors are now warned away from this park because it is so full of land mines. Not only are the mines a danger to visitors but they are injuring and killing the elephants that step on them.

Although tourism is intended to be one of the most important parts of Mozambique's economy in the future, the big question is whether there is enough wildlife left in Gorongosa to attract visitors. Conservation is often on the minds of younger tourists,

Left inset: Panthera Azul offers weekly bus service between Maputo and Johannesburg, South Africa. Perhaps if the fence that separates Kruger National Park (above) from Mozambique is removed, more wildlife (right inset) will inhabit the area.

especially those who travel lightly, with just a backpack full of their belongings. Rather than driving cars, they prefer to arrive on the Panthera Azul, a bus service that runs twice a week between Johannesburg and Maputo.

There has been talk of removing a long fence that separates Kruger National Park in South Africa from the adjacent wildlife area in Mozambique. This would allow the wildlife to migrate more naturally in the region and would help reestablish this important wildlife area. The wildlife areas of Mozambique have the greatest potential for tourism, which is the country's biggest hope right now for employment and income. It will take much longer for Mozambique's factories and industries to be rebuilt.

Villagers get water from a pump made in India and donated by Norway.

MOZAMBIQUE'S FUTURE

For the first time in the history of independent Mozambique, the country has a unique opportunity for success. With the end of apartheid in South Africa and the election of its first black president, Nelson Mandela, Mozambique has a powerful and friendly neighbor. South Africa is the major economic power in the entire southern Africa region and will have a strong impact on Mozambique's economic growth.

There are an estimated 600,000 to 1 million Portuguese-speaking people in South Africa. When the Portuguese left Mozambique at the time of independence, many of them traveled the short distance to South Africa. Others came later to escape the civil war. The rest came from other former Portuguese colonies. Former Mozambicans retained strong ties to Mozambique and are now investing in its rebuilding. Because most of the education and training was given to white people, they have the skills that

Mozambique needs, and the black government would like some of them to come back. Until it can educate its own people, the country needs these white, Portuguese-speaking businesspeople, teachers, doctors, and engineers.

Mozambique's other neighbors are Zimbabwe, Malawi, Swaziland, Zambia, and Tanzania. All are peaceful, stable countries, with their own struggles for independence behind them. They played important roles as places of refuge for Mozambique's people who fled their homes during the worst years of the civil war.

FREE AND FAIR ELECTIONS

Although the war had come to an end and people were returning to Mozambique, there remained a large and difficult question. How could this war-ravaged country pull itself together and hold democratic elections? With a population that is still largely illiterate, with so little in the way of communications, with roads yet to be repaired, was it possible to hold fair elections?

The dramatic transformation of Mozambique to a country at peace and on the road to democracy was accomplished with a combination of intelligent planning, a strong presence of UN troops overseeing the disarming of the soldiers from both sides, and the nature of the Mozambique people themselves.

A three-week political campaign preceded the two days of elections on October 27-28, 1994. There were more than seven thousand polling stations throughout the country, each one set up to handle one thousand voters.

When the voting was complete, 5.4 million people, about 85 percent of all the registered voters, had actually voted. That is

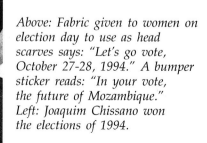

Above: Fabric given to women on election day to use as head scarves says: "Let's go vote, October 27-28, 1994." A bumper sticker reads: "In your vote, the future of Mozambique." Left: Joaquim Chissano won the elections of 1994.

much higher than the percentage of people who vote in presidential elections in the United States. The ballots listed more than a dozen political parties, each one showing the face of the person running for president. Each party also was represented by a symbol, since many of the voters could not read. Only people who were living in the country were allowed to vote; there were no absentee ballots.

It took time to count all the paper ballots, but in the end the results were agreed upon by the two principal parties, Frelimo and Renamo. President Joaquim Chissano won the election with 53.3 percent of the vote. His closest opponent, Afonso Dhlakama of Renamo, received 33.73 percent.

The voters also chose 250 people to represent them in Parliament. Frelimo's party received 129 seats and Renamo 112; the remaining 9 seats were divided up among some of the smaller parties that participated in the election. The close vote for Parliamentary seats has created a government with two strong parties, a rarity in African politics.

On December 8 the new members of Parliament were sworn into office and the following day, December 9, President Chissano took the oath of office. His term is for five years—until 1999.

MOZAMBIQUE AND THE WORLD

With peaceful countries all around it and the war over, with successful elections now a part of its history, Mozambique's people now face the tremendous task of rebuilding their country, the economy, and their lives.

Much of the economy has been based on aid; the United States, for example, gave about $70 million in direct and indirect aid in

Schoolchildren buy snacks in their school yard.

The old ways will continue as Mozambique rushes into the future.

1994. Diplomatic relations between the two countries are excellent. Trade and economic growth have increased during the same period, with South Africa exporting more than $200 million worth of goods to Mozambique in 1994.

Without the dramatic change in South Africa that brought Nelson Mandela to power as president, Mozambique's chances for success would be greatly reduced. Shortly after he was elected, President Mandela chose to make his first official visit to Mozambique. Now with this powerful country as an ally, Mozambique can count on South Africa's economic strength to bolster its own economy.

On June 25, 1995, Mozambique marks the twentieth anniversary of its independence from Portugal with real prospects for creating a good life for its people who have suffered so much, so long.

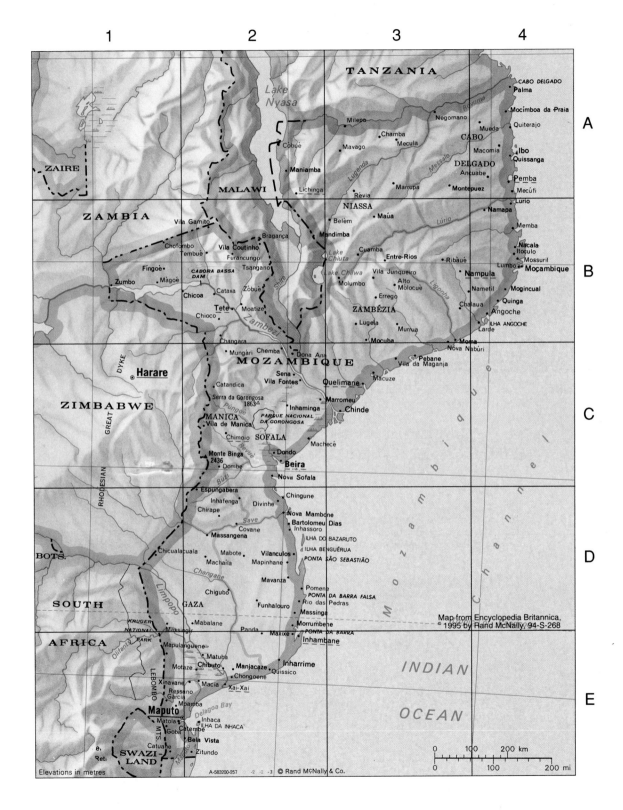

1   2   3   4

TANZANIA

CABO DELGADO
Palma

Mocímboa da Praia

Negomano

Milepa

Chamba
Mecula

Quiterajo

Mueda

Mavago

CABO

Macomia

Ibo
Quissanga

Maniamba

Marrupa

DELGADO

Ancuabe

Pemba

Lichinga

Rêvia

Montepuez

Mecúfi

Cóbuè

MALAWI

NIASSA

Lúrio

Namapa

ZAMBIA

Vila Gamito

Belém

Maúa

Memba

Bragança

Mandimba

Nacala

Vila Coutinho

Cuamba

Itoculo

Chofombo
Tembuè

Furancungo

Lake
Chiuta

Entre-Rios

Ribàuè

Mossuril

Tsangano

Lumbo

Moçambique

Fíngoè

CABORA BASSA
DAM

Zóbuè

Lake Chilwa

Vila Junqueiro

Nampula

Zumbo

Màgoè

Molumbo

Alto
Molocuè

Nametil

Mogincual

Chicoa

Cataxa

Tete

Moatize

Errego

Chalaua

Quinga

Chioco

ZAMBÉZIA

Angoche

Lugela

Murrua

Larde

ILHA ANGOCHE

Changara

Mocuba

Moma

Mungàri
Chemba

Dona Ana

Nova Nabúri

MOZAMBIQUE

Harare

Sena
Vila Fontes

Pebane
Vila da Maganja

Catandica

Quelimane

Macuze

ZIMBABWE

Serra da Gorongosa
1863

Marromeu

MANICA
Vila de Manica

Inhaminga

Chinde

PARQUE NACIONAL
DA GORONGOSA

Chimoio

SOFALA

Dondo

Machecè

Monte Binga
2436

Dombe

Beira

Nova Sofala

BOTS.

Espungabera

Chingune

Inhafenga

Divinhe

Chirape

Nova Mambone

Covane

Bartolomeu Dias
Inhassoro

Massangena

ILHA DO BAZARUTO

Chicualacuala

Mabote

Vilanculos

ILHA BENGUÉRUA

Machaila

Mapinhane

PONTA SÃO SEBASTIÃO

Mavanza

SOUTH

GAZA

Chigubo

Funhalouro

Pomene
PONTA DA BARRA FALSA
Rio das Pedras

Mabalane

Massinga

AFRICA

Panda

Morrumbene
PONTA DA BARRA

KRUGER
NATIONAL
PARK

Massingir

Maxixe

Inhambane

Mapulanguene

Matuba

Chibuto

Manjacaze

Inharrime

Motaze

Chongoene

Quissico

Xinavane

Macia

Xai-Xai

Ressano
Garcia

Mpamba

Maputo

Delagoa Bay

Matola

Inhaca
ILHA DA INHACA

Catembe

Goba

Bela Vista

Catuane

Zitundo

SWAZI-
LAND

INDIAN

OCEAN

Map from Encyclopedia Britannica,
© 1995 by Rand McNally. 94-S-268

0   100   200 km

0   100   200 mi

Elevations in metres

A-583200-257   -2   -2   -3   © Rand McNally & Co.

A

B

C

D

E

MAP KEY

Alto Molocue — B3
Ancuabe — A4
Angoche — B4
Angoche, Ilha, *island* — B4
Bartolomeu Dias — D2
Bazaruto, Ilha do, *island* — D2
Beira — C2
Bela Vista — E2
Belem — B3
Benguerua, Ilha — D2
Braganca — B2
Buzi, river — C2, D2
Cabo Delgado,
  province — A3, A4, B3, B4
Cabora Bassa Dam — B2
Cantandica — C2
Cantaxa — B2
Catembe — E1
Catuane — E1
Chalaua — B3
Chamba — A3
Changane, *river* — D1, D2, E2
Changara — B2
Chemba — C2
Chibuto — E2
Chicoa — B2
Chicualacuala — D1
Chigubo — D2
Chilwa, Lake — B2
Chimoio — C2
Chinde — C3
Chingune — D2
Chioco — B2
Chirape — D2
Chiuta, Lake — B2, B3
Chofombo — B1
Chongoene — E2
Cobue — A2
Coutinho, Vila — B2
Covane — D2
Cuamba — B3
Delagoa Bay — E2
Delgado, Cabo, *cape* — A4
Divinhe — D2
Dombe — C2
Dona Ana — C2
Dondo — C2
Entre-Rios — B3
Errego — B3
Espungabera — D2
Fingoe — B1
Fontes, Vila — C2
Funhalouro — D2
Furancungo — B2
Gamito, Vila — B2
Gaza, *province* — D1, D2, E1, E2
Goba — E1
Ibo — A4
Indian Ocean — E2, E3, E4

Inhaca — E2
Inhaca, Ilha da — E2
Inhafenga — D2
Inhambane — E2
Inhaminga — C2
Inharrime — E2
Inhassoro — D2
Itoculo — B4
Junquiero, Vila — B3
Larde — B4
Lichinga — A2
Ligonha, *river* — B3
Limpopo, *river* — D1, D2, E2
Lugela — B3
Lugenda, *river* — A3, B3
Lumbo — B4
Lurio — B4
Lurio, *river* — B3, B4
Mabalane — D2
Mabote — D2
Machaila — D2
Machece — C2
Macia — E2
Macomia — A4
Macuze — C3
Maganja, Vila da — C3
Magoe — B1
Mandimba — B2
Maniamba — A2
Manica, *province* — C2, D2
Manica, Vila de — C2
Manjacaze — E2
Mapinhane — D2
Mapulanguene — E1
Maputo — E1
Maputo, *river* — E1, E2
Marromeu — C2
Marrupa — A3
Massangena — D2
Massinga — D2
Massingir — D1
Matola — E1
Matuba — E2
Maua — B3
Mavago — A3
Mavanza — D2
Maxixe — E2
Mbamba — E1
Mecufi — A4
Mecula — A3
Memba — B4
Messalo, *river* — A3, A4
Milepa — A3
Moatize — B2
Mocambique — B4
Mocimboa da Praia — A4
Mocuba — B3
Mogincual — B4
Molumbo — B3

Moma — B3
Monte Binga, *peak* — C2
Montepuez — A3
Morrumbene — D2
Mossuril — B4
Motaze — E2
Mozambique Channel
  A4, B4, C2, C3, C4, D2, D3, D4
Mueda — A4
Mungari — C2
Murrua — B3
Nacala — B4
Namapa — B4
Nametil — B3
Nampula — B3
Negomano — A3
Niassa, *province* — A2, A3, B2, B3
Nova Mambone — D2
Nova Naburi — B3
Nova Sofala — C2
Nyasa, Lake — A2, B2
Olifants, *river* — D1, E1, E2
Palma — A4
Panda — E2
Parque Nacional da Gorongosa — C2
Pebane — C3
Pemba — A4
Pomene — D2
Ponta da Barra — D2, E2
Ponta da Barra Falsa — D2
Ponta Sao Sebastiao — D2
Pungoe, *river* — C2
Quelimane — C3
Quinga — B4
Quissanga — A4
Quissico — E2
Quiterajo — A4
Ressano Garcia — E1
Revia — A3
Revue, *river* — C2
Ribaue — B3
Rio das Pedras — D2
Rovuma, *river* — A3, A4
Save, *river* — D2
Sena — C2
Serra da Gorongosa, *peak* — C2
Shire, *river* — B2, C2
Sofala, *province* — B2, C2, C3, D2
Tembue — B2
Tete — B2
Tsangano — B2
Vilanculos — D2
Xai-Xai — E2
Xinavane — E2
Zambezi, *river* — B2, C2, C3
Zambezia,
  province — B1, B2, B3, C2, C3
Zitundo — E2
Zobue — B2
Zumbo — B1

MINI FACTS AT A GLANCE

GENERAL INFORMATION

Official Name: *República de Moçambique* (Republic of Mozambique)

Capital: Maputo, formerly known as Lourenço Marques

Government: According to the 1990 constitution, Mozambique is a multiparty democratic republic with a single legislative house, Assembly of the Republic. The Assembly members are elected by universal, direct, adult vote. The president, who is chief of state and head of government, is directly elected for a five-year term. The 1990 constitution also recognizes other political parties.

Religion: There is no official religion in Mozambique and the constitution guarantees freedom of religion to everyone. An estimated 10 percent of the people are Muslims and about 20 to 30 percent identify themselves as Christians. Some two-thirds of Mozambicans follow traditional religious practices. Many people who are officially part of a Christian or Islamic group also retain their traditional religious beliefs.

Ethnic Composition: Almost all Mozambicans are of Black African origin. There are some sixty distinct ethnic groups including Makua, Tsonga, Shona, Yao, Swahili, and Makonde. A small number of Portuguese, Arabs, and other Europeans live in the cities.

Language: Portuguese is the language of government and business. Many people speak their own language as well as Portuguese. The most widely spoken languages include Tsonga and the Macua-Lomue group of languages. Yao and Makonde are spoken in the country's far north. Shona/Shangaan speakers live on Zimbabwe's border. All these languages are spoken by many other people in neighboring countries. Swahili, a mixture of African and Arabic languages, is spoken by a large number of people, especially along the coast. Some English is spoken, mainly for business activities.

National Flag: The flag consists of three broad horizontal stripes of green, black, and yellow, separated by narrow bands of white. A red triangle extends from the hoist; a yellow five-pointed star is centered on the triangle. A white book is placed on the star over which is shown a hoe and a rifle. The rifle represents defense and vigilance, the book represents education, and the hoe represents agriculture.

National Anthem: "Viva Viva Frelimo"

Money: The metical (mt.) is the official currency. In 1993 one metical was worth $0.00022 in United States currency.

Membership in International Organizations: African Development Bank (AfDB); General Agreement on Tariffs and Trade (GATT); International Monetary Fund (IMF); Nonaligned Movement (NAM); Organization of African Unity (OAU); Preferential Trade Area for Eastern and Southern African States; Southern African Development Community (SADC); United Nations (UN)

Weights and Measures: The metric system is in use.

Population: Estimated 1994 population 17,417,000; density of population 56 persons per sq. mi. (22 persons per sq km); 66 percent rural, 34 percent urban

Cities:

Maputo	931,600
Beira	298,800
Nampula	250,500
Quelimane	146,200
Nacala	125,200
Tete	112,200
Chimoio	108,800

(Population based on 1991 estimates.)

GEOGRAPHY

Border: Mozambique is bordered by Tanzania in the north; Malawi, Zambia, Zimbabwe, South Africa, and Swaziland in the west; and by South Africa in the south. The Indian Ocean marks the country's entire eastern boundary.

Coastline: Mozambique's southeastern coastline of 1,556 mi. (2,504 km) stretches along the Indian Ocean. The irregularly shaped coastline has many natural harbors.

Land: The Zambezi River divides the country into two halves—the lowlands in the south and the highlands in the north. Nearly half of the land is low-lying, marshy, flat plain. The swampy and marshy land is a good breeding ground for insects such as mosquitoes and tsetse flies that carry sleeping sickness. The lowlands support some 70 percent of Mozambique's population. The western region along the border contains highlands. The Bazaruto Archipelago, made of five small islands, is south of Beira off the coast. The islands are designated as a national park.

Highest Point: Mount Binga, 7,992 ft. (2,436 m)

Lowest Point: Sea level

Rivers and Lakes: Some sixty rivers run through Mozambique from west to east to the Indian Ocean. The major rivers are the Zambezi and Save in the center, the Lurio in the north, and the Limpopo in the south. In the swampy areas, rivers make it more difficult for people to move across the country. Some rivers dry up completely during the dry season.

Lake Malawi, also called Lake Nyasa, is one of the larger bodies of water in Africa. Located on the northeastern border, this navigable lake is shared by Mozambique, Malawi, and Tanzania. Lake Cabora Bassa was formed by the Cabora Bassa Dam, which is constructed on the Zambezi River. Several other rivers have small hydroelectric dams.

Forests: About half of the land is covered with forests, scrub, and woodlands. The wet regions support thick forests, but the drier interiors support only a thin savanna vegetation. Hardwoods, such as ebony, flourish throughout the country. The northwestern highlands support a dense tropical vegetation of ironwood, palm, and ebony while the drier interior lowlands support a thin grass and scrub vegetation. Mangroves and coconut palms are common along the coasts. Many conifers and eucalyptus areas are being replanted under reforestation projects.

Wildlife: Mozambique's wildlife includes elephants, buffaloes, wildebeests, zebras, lions, spotted hyena, hippopotamuses, crocodiles, and some 300 varieties of birds. The 5,000 sq. mi. (12,950 sq. km) Gorongosa Game Reserve was a major tourist attraction with its great herds of buffaloes, lions, elephants, hippos, and kudos before it closed down in 1973 because of civil war. Tourists are not allowed in the

Maputo Elephant Park, famous for its herds of elephants, as it is strewn with land mines. The wildlife areas of Mozambique have the greatest potential for tourism.

Climate: The tropical climate has two distinct seasons—dry and wet. The wet season is from October through March, and the dry season lasts from April to November. More than 80 percent of the entire year's rain falls during the wet season. Most areas receive between 47 to 79 in. (120 to 200 cm) of rainfall. The average annual rainfall is greatest over the western hills and the central areas, and lowest in the southwest. Drought is frequent, especially in the south. Extreme variation in rainfall can result in widespread famine. There is a little variation in temperatures from north to south. Temperatures range from 68° F (20° C) in July to 85° F (29° C) in January.

Greatest Distance: North to South: 1,100 mi. (1,770 km)
East to West: 680 mi. (1,094 km)

Area: 308,642 sq. mi. (799,380 sq. km)

ECONOMY AND INDUSTRY

Agriculture: Some 80 percent of people in Mozambique are farmers, but less than 5 percent of land is actually under cultivation. The land is not particularly rich and the farming methods are very basic. Most of the farmers work the land by hand with few tools and oxen. The variation in rainfall makes irrigation very important in most areas. Severe drought resulted in a crop failure in the early 1980s. The chief cash crops are cotton, cashew nuts, sisal, sugarcane, and tea. For local use, farmers grow cassava, maize, millet, rice, sorghum, fruits, bananas, coconuts, oilseeds, potatoes, and some rice.

Fishing: Fishing has always been a way of life for many Mozambicans. Both ocean and river waters are rich in fish and shrimp. Mackerel, marlin, sailfish, swordfish, hammerhead shark, anchovies, and prawns (shrimp) are the principal fish caught. Fishing accounts for about one-fifth of all exports.

Mining: There are enormous deposits of coal, beryllium, and limestone. Mozambique is thought to have the world's largest reserve of tantalite—a mineral used in producing electricity. Other minerals include iron ore, zirconium, asbestos, uranium, copper, nickel, gold, diamonds, emeralds, apatite, bauxite, fluorite, graphite, and magnetite. Reserves of natural gas are found in great quantities in Inhambane Province. There are no known sources of petroleum and the country imports all of its petroleum requirements.

Electrical energy is primarily derived from hydroelectric power and coal. The multipurpose Cahora Bassa Dam and power complex is one of the largest hydroelectric projects in Africa. Mozambique exports hydroelectricity to South Africa.

Manufacturing: The chief manufacturing sectors are textiles, plastics, beverages, food and fruit processing (chiefly sugar, tea, wheat, flour), chemicals (vegetable oil, oil cakes, soap, paints), cement, glass, and asbestos. Cashew nuts are processed for overseas markets.

Transportation: Mozambique's roads and railways, running west to east, connect its landlocked neighbors to seaports on the Indian Ocean. Most railway lines do not connect with each other (north to south) anywhere in the country. In the early 1990s there were 1,857 mi. (2,988 km) of railroad tracks. A coastal road runs along the length of Mozambique, but there are very few roads in the interior. Many small unpaved roads can be used only in the dry season. Mozambique has a total of 16,955 mi. (27,286 km) of roads, of which roughly 20 percent are paved. Mozambique's state-owned airline, Linhas Aereas de Moçambique (LAM), offers international service. International airports are at Maputo and Beira.

Mozambique's excellent port facilities are used by neighboring landlocked countries. Maputo, Beira, and Nacala are the chief ports. The Maputo port can handle the largest freighters with modern cargo hoisting devices. The Beira port is designed to accommodate shipments of coal and to allow oil freighters to tie up and unload oil. Nacala's modern facilities make it one of the highest-rated ports along the East African Coast. The strategically important Beira Corridor gets its name from a triple transportation link—railroad, road, and pipeline—that extends from the Zimbabwe border to the port of Beira.

Communication: Most of the telecommunication services are government operated. In the early 1990s there was one radio receiver per 30 persons; one television set per 424 persons, and one telephone per 211 persons.

Trade: The chief imports are food items, equipment, machinery and spare parts, petroleum and petroleum products, and consumer goods. The major import sources are South Africa, the United States, Portugal, and Italy. The chief export items are shrimp, cashew nuts, cotton, sugar, and timber. The major export destinations are Spain, the United States, Japan, and Portugal.

EVERYDAY LIFE

Health: At independence in 1975 the government banned private practice by doctors and most of the country's 550 fully trained doctors left Mozambique. Medical care is without charge and the country has a nationalized health care system. Since independence the government has been stressing improved sanitation, extensive vaccination programs, and preventive and rural medicine. There is a shortage of medical supplies and trained personnel as most of the clinics established by the government for primary care were destroyed during the civil war. Sleeping sickness, caused by the tsetse fly, and malaria are the two biggest threats to health. In the early 1990s there was one physician per 44,000 persons and one hospital bed per 1,300 persons.

Life expectancy at 47 years for males and 50 years for females is low. Infant mortality rate at 130 per 1,000 is among the highest in the world.

Education: At independence almost 90 percent of population could not read or write. In the early 1980s there was a major emphasis on campaigns for adult literacy and other adult education. With the purpose of increasing the skilled workforce, the government operates several training schools for electricians and maritime schools for seamen. The Eduardo Mondlane University at Maputo is the country's only institution of higher learning. All university students are required to give the same number of years of public service as they have spent at the university. Education at all levels is free; primary schooling lasts for five years and secondary schooling for seven years, comprising two cycles of two and five years. In the early 1990s the literacy rate was about 33 percent.

Holidays:
New Year's Day, January 1
Heroes' Day, February 3
Women's Day, April 7
Workers' Day, May 1
Independence Day, June 25
Anniversary of the End of Armed Struggle, September 7
Anniversary of the Opening of Armed Struggle, September 25
Family Day, December 25

Culture: Sculpture is the traditional art in Mozambique. The complex "family trees" carved in ebony by Makonde people are one of the best examples of Mozambique sculpture. Rock paintings of Mount Binga in Manica Province give a clue to early life in Mozambique. The Nambu Productions, a performing arts company, and a national dance company promote contemporary art forms based on the traditional culture. Storytellers are an important part of Mozambique's oral tradition.

The National Library at Maputo is the largest library in the country with a sizeable collection of books. Major museums in Maputo are the Museum of Natural History, specializing in natural history and ethnography; the Freire de Andrade Museum for minerals; and the military History Museum. There is a museum of marine biology at Ilha da Inhaca.

Society: The civil war had disastrous effects on the Mozambique people. Some 3 million were displaced by the conflict and another 1.5 million people were forced to leave their families and villages and take refuge in neighboring countries. At the end of the civil war people came back to the war-torn countryside where most of the infrastructure was badly damaged. Large numbers of war wounded and orphan children were rehabilitated and cared for after Frelimo took over. Equal rights were given to women, and they were given positions in the party and government.

Crafts: People make baskets, mats, pestles to grind meal, axes, hoes, and cooking utensils out of wood, cane, sisal, and shells. Tapestries made in Zambezia province and shell ornaments made in Nampula Province are among the most admired crafts.

Tourism: Mozambique's beach resorts are favored by South Africans and other neighboring countries. Costa do Sol is a favored destination of beach goers from surrounding landlocked countries. Offshore coral reefs, flamingoes, dolphins, birds, and exotic fish are the main pull for tourism.

Sports and Recreation: Mozambicans are great sports fans, especially of soccer. Mozambique has some of the best runners in the world. Musical instruments include wooden drums; *lupembe,* a wind instrument made either of animal horn or wood or gourd; and *marimba* (xylophone). Modern popular *marrabenta* music is based on traditional complex African rhythms. Dancing always has been a form of communication and expression for African people. *Mapiko* dance comes from the north, *tufo* is from the Mozambique Island, and the *nhau* is from Tete Province.

Social Welfare: Most social welfare is done either on individual, family, or charitable organization basis. People tend to take care of their older relatives at home.

IMPORTANT DATES

A.D. 100s—Bantu-speakers are settled in Mozambique

800s—Arabs also live in the area

1498—Vasco da Gama, the Portuguese explorer, stops at Delagoa Bay (modern Maputo)

1505—Portuguese establish a trading post

1510—Portuguese are in control of trade in Mozambique

1515—Portuguese exploration of the interior begins

1531—Portuguese establish two inland trading settlements

1544—Portuguese establish a post on the coast at Quelimane

1752—The first Portuguese colonial governor is appointed

1790—An estimated 9,000 slaves were being sent out of Mozambique every year

1833—The Zulu capture the fort at the town of Lourenço Marques

1844—A treaty is signed between Britain and Portugal to halt the slave trade

1875—A dispute between the British and the Portuguese is settled in favor of Portugal

1878—Portugal outlaws the slave trade; the Native Labor Code gives Africans the right to choose whether they want to work for Europeans

1879—The British are defeated at the Battle of Isandhlwana by the Zulu

1885-86—A conference is held in Berlin to settle European claims over African land; Mozambique is recognized as a Portuguese colony

1886—Gold is discovered in South Africa

1891—Portugal agrees to Britain's claim over the region of Mashonaland; Mozambique's present-day borders are established

1895—The Portuguese establish control over the southern part of Mozambique

1898—Lourenço Marques (modern Maputo) becomes the capital

1907—The Portuguese move the administration of the Mozambique colony from Lisbon to district offices in Mozambique

1909—The Portuguese make a deal about black Mozambican miners with South Africa

1912—The Portuguese set up trading posts in Mozambique

1917—An uprising takes place against the Portuguese policy of making Africans fight against the Germans

1930—The Colonial Act ends a period of limited autonomy for Mozambique

1951—Mozambique becomes an overseas province of Portugal

1961—The National Library is founded

1962—Three liberation groups merge to form *Frente de Libertacao de Moçambique* (Frelimo); work on Cabora Bassa, the huge hydroelectric dam, begins with foreign investments; Mozambique's first university opens in Maputo

1964—Frelimo launches its first attack against the Portuguese

1968—António Salazar is replaced by Marcelo Caetano as prime minister of Portugal

1972—Cashew production reaches an all time high of 216,000 tons (196,000 metric tons)

1974—An army coup in Portugal opens the way for independence in Mozambique

1975—Mozambique becomes an independent people's republic; white settlers continue to flee the country; some 118,000 Mozambique men are working in South African mines; after independence some 40,000 whites remain in Mozambique

1976—Mozambique closes the border with Rhodesia; all private homes and buildings are nationalized; Lourenço Marques, the capital city, is renamed Maputo; *Resistência Nacional Moçambicana* or Mozambican National Resistance (Renamo) is formed

1977—The Treaty of Friendship and Cooperation is signed with the former Soviet Union; relations with Portugal deteriorate; Portuguese nationals are expelled

1978—Banks are nationalized; Mozambican mine workers are paid wages at a better rate

1979—Fifteen Catholic missions are ordered to close; the Southern African Development Co-Ordination Conference is founded, which later becomes Southern African Development Community

1980—The metical is adopted as the unit of currency in place of the escudo; the Cabora Bassa Dam is completed

1981—Television is introduced

1982—Cashew production reaches a low of 18,000 tons (16,000 metric tons)

1983—The current version of the national flag is adopted

1984—Mozambique joins the International Monetary Fund and the World Bank; the Nkomati Accord is reached with South Africa

1985—Free enterprise is encouraged in the limited sectors of the economy

1986—Renamo declares war on Zimbabwe; Samora Machel, the head of Frelimo, dies in a plane crash

1987—Rebel activities lead to severe food shortages and increase the number of Mozambican refugees outside the country; an Economic Rehabilitation Program is launched; Joaquim Chissano receives outside help in his fight against the rebels

1988—Renamo blows several hundred pylons that carry electricity from the Cabora Bassa Dam; amnesty for Renamo members results in more than 3,000 rebel defections

1989—Frelimo abandons its Marxist-Leninist ideology; South Africa claims that the government has cut off all aid to Renamo

1990—A new constitution is adopted; the country's name is changed to the Republic of Mozambique; the government and Renamo sign a partial cease-fire

1992—Renamo and Frelimo sign the General Peace Agreement in Rome, Italy; Mozambique becomes a full member of General Agreement on Tariffs and Trade; inflation reaches a record 50 percent

1993—Renamo leader Afonso Dhlakama agrees to turn over territory under his control to the Frelimo government; the government agrees to appoint three Renamo officials from each of the country's ten provinces; Denmark and Great Britain grant loans to finance health and agriculture

1994—Mozambique holds its first multiparty democratic elections and Chissano remains president

IMPORTANT PEOPLE

Dr. Aldo Ajello, United Nation's special representative; worked with both Frelimo and Renamo leaders to establish assembly points for their soldiers after cease-fire agreement was reached in the early 1990s

Pieter Willem Botha (1916-   ), president of South Africa (1984- 1989); agreed to stop support to Renamo

Samora Moises Machel (1933-86); the first president of independent Mozambique

Chissano, sculptor; works in wood; his work depicts the struggle of the century through human figures

Joaquim Alberto Chissano (1939-   ), a Frelimo leader; interim president during the transitional period leading up to independence of Mozambique; became foreign minister in 1975; also succeeded Machel as president in 1986; reelected in 1994

Hastings Banda (?-1994), president of Malawi from 1966 to 1994

Mia Couto (1955-   ), poet and novelist; work includes *Sleepwalking Land,* and *Voices Made Night;* he has been called the "Dreamer of Memories"

José Craveirinha (1922-   ), author and poet; defends Portuguese as the official language

Afonso Dhlakama, leader of Renamo, the opposition party to Frelimo; his policies caused heavy destruction in the Mozambique countryside

Dingane, brother of Zulu leader Shaka

Luis Bernardo Honwana (1942-   ), writer and documentary filmmaker; work includes *We Killed Mangy-Dog*

Frederik Willem de Klerk (1936-   ), president of South Africa (1989-1993); ended apartheid and made black majority rule possible

Malangatana, artist famous for outdoor murals; paints about colonial period and the civil war

Nelson Rohihlahla Mandela (1918-   ), South African lawyer and black nationalist; South Africa's first black president (1993)

Eduardo C. Mondlane (1920-69), leader of Frelimo; he was educated in South Africa and abroad; he also worked at the United Nations in New York

Maria Mutola, the best-known runner in the country; she was presented a special gold medal by President Chissano for her achievements

Nkatunga, the best-known Makonde sculptor who depicts daily life in the rural community

Julius Kambarage Nyerere (1922-   ), the first president of Tanzania (1964); his efforts led to the founding of Frelimo in 1962

Noémia De Sousa (1926-   ), author; has been called "mother" of the Mozambican writers

Shaka, powerful warrior and leader of Zulu people

Compiled by Chandrika Kaul

INDEX

Page numbers that appear in boldface type indicate illustrations

About the Authors

Jason Lauré was born in Chehalis, Washington, and lived in California before joining the United States army and serving in France. He attended Columbia University and worked for *The New York Times.* He traveled to San Francisco and became a photographer during the turbulent 1960s. Mr. Lauré recorded those events before setting out on the first of many trips to Africa.

Mr. Lauré covers the political life of that continent and also has made a number of expeditions across the Sahara. He has written about, and photographed in, forty countries in Africa.

In the Enchantment of the World series, Mr. Lauré has written books on Zimbabwe, Bangladesh, Angola, Zambia, Namibia, and Botswana and has collaborated on Tanzania with Ettagale Blauer.

Mr. Lauré is married to Marisia Lauré, a translator. Mr. Lauré is based in New York and spends half of each year in Africa. They have a daughter, Mirella, born on November 9, 1994.

Ettagale Blauer has been writing about Africa for young adult readers for twenty years. She has written three books, published by Farrar, Straus & Giroux Inc., on South Africa, Portugal, and Bangladesh, in collaboration with Jason Lauré. Their Bangladesh book was nominated for the National Book Award. In the Enchantment of the World series, she has written *Tanzania* in collaboration with Jason Lauré.

Ms. Blauer has traveled widely in Africa, including a year in South Africa and a three-month-long overland trip from Morocco to Kenya. She has visited many diamond and gold mines during her research and says she knows the continent "from beneath the ground and up."

Born in New York City, Ms. Blauer was graduated from Hunter College with a degree in creative writing. Ms. Blauer also is well known in the field of jewelry writing and is the author of *Contemporary American Jewelry Design.*